The Winning Option

The Winning Option

Ralph T. Dames

Nelson-Hall nh Chicago

Library of Congress Cataloging in Publication Data

Dames, Ralph Theodore, 1927-
The winning option.

Bibliography: p.
Includes index.
1. Put and call transactions. I. Title.
HG6041.D34   332.6'45   79-23369
ISBN 0-88229-527-6

Copyright © 1980 by Ralph T. Dames

Manufactured in the United States of America

10 9 8 7 6 5 4 3 2 1

Contents

Preface

I firmly believe that most Americans harbor the dream of joining that select group called the *nouveau riche.* Instant wealth, however obtained, is almost always an elusive goal, and yet for many this dream of utopia is the only element that separates hope from despair.

Legalized casino gambling appears to be a new wave for the future, having already moved to the East Coast from the deserts of Nevada. I tend to agree with the sociologists who assess this trend as a manifestation of individual frustration with inflation, taxes, and a host of other suppressing factors that dominate our daily life but over which one has practically no control. Hard work coupled with a savings account seldom leads to financial security, much less to the good life. Is it any wonder that Lady Luck is not only a welcome diversion but also an attractive substitute for the work ethic?

In the investment world there is often a similar feeling of helplessness when the small investor attempts to play within the system. More often than not, the Little Guy investor ends up a losing participant. But where is the Little Guy's investment casino? It cannot be the traditional Wall Street stock exchanges: the time constant for success and the odds of winning certainly negate that possibility. I contend that the answer lies in the stock options market. Here the option trader, like the successful gambler, must be disciplined, determined, patient and, at times, daring if he is to come away a big winner. A more definitive guide for pursuing this goal is presented in the following chapters. I consider the approach outlined to be the winning option among investment alternatives.

A number of individuals were most helpful throughout preparation of the manuscript. Special thanks go to Ms. Melanie Holmes and Mr. Jack Nagel, who reviewed the entire manuscript and offered many valuable comments and suggestions. Of course without the encouragement and labor of immediate family there would have been no end result. Here my wife Katherine served admirably in both categories. Joe Pussy, my other close associate, performed in typical feline fashion. His encouragement was somewhat more subtle, however, as he clocked more time sleeping on the manuscript than I spent preparing it.

1

Breaking Tradition

This book is written for the small investor who consistently loses in the stock market while steadfastly believing he can strike it rich. It's for the individual with a basic knowledge of market operation whose investment capital never grows beyond the awkward stage. The dollar value is too small to attract much more than cursory attention at the brokerage den, but large enough to call Missing Persons if it runs away from home. This is the investor who would never seriously consider seeking professional money management because, right or wrong, he's generally comfortable serving as his own investment counselor. But being familiar with the rule book and developing his own game plan is not enough. He seldom wins the game.

Many reasons have been given why the Little Guy rarely succeeds. These explanations cover a broad spectrum, from his highly emotional approach to investing, to the so-called Wall Street conspiracy. But perhaps the simplest answer,

1

and the one closest to the truth, is that the small investor is competing in a money game against seasoned professionals. These floor traders, market specialists, and money managers play the game with much better odds than the Little Guy. Their winning edge is provided by a combination of advantages ranging from lower, if any, commissions to a much more timely and thorough access to market information. I believe that for these reasons any Little Guy approach to investing based on a knowledge of business fundamentals is eventually doomed to failure.

Fortunately, with a certain amount of discipline, the odds of a small investor succeeding on Wall Street can be significantly improved. The purpose of this book is to present an approach to the market that can produce exceptional returns while minimizing the risk of prolonged and heavy losses. This method, like all others, is not foolproof, but it is relatively easy to use, reasonably well defined, and at least for me, has been highly successful.

The basic principle that underlies this investment philosophy is simply stated: Stay away from the stock market and only risk investment capital in the options market at the most opportune times. Hopefully, the reader is already familiar with stock options, especially call options. These are contracts to purchase 100 shares of a given stock at a specified price during a fixed period of time. A description of this fast-growing market is given in chapter 5. For now I will say that mechanically the options market is similar to the stock market but with much greater leverage and associated risks.

That's right, don't buy stocks! If this advice sounds radical or un-American then you're either satisfied with your stock market performance or perhaps you're a member of the Wall Street establishment. As for myself, I'm not in either category, and I suspect that expounding my market approach won't exactly endear me to the brokerage community.

In the past few years a number of potentially successful investment strategies involving the use of options have surfaced. Many are highly computerized. Also, with a number of these strategies the attempt to minimize risk puts a cap on rewards. This in turn prohibits a large return unless correspondingly large sums of money are invested. The strategy discussed in this book does not particularly suffer from these constraints and warrants at least equal consideration with other methods. However, in the final analysis, the reader must decide for himself which investment vehicle or technique is personally appropriate and suited to his needs.

In setting forth my market philosophy, I speak not only to the small investor, but also as a bona fide Little Guy who, for many years, chased those Merrill Lynch bulls across the TV screen toward greener pastures. The bulls never stopped running, and neither did my market losses until I discovered a better way. It should also be stated up front that my investment philosophy is not based on decades of experience as an investment counselor or floor trader. I consider this to be an asset. I'm not biased by the privileged inner workings of Wall Street to which the small investor is never privy, nor am I out to gather a paying clientele who might be more impressed with market savvy than results. Actually, the greatest advantage the Little Guy can have is to recognize he is a Little Guy, with limited resources and even less knowledge of what can and will make the market move. As soon as one recognizes and accepts this fact, it makes investment planning a lot simpler and considerably less work. It may sound contradictory, but I believe this is one of the few areas of endeavor where less work can lead to greater success.

If one follows the method explained in subsequent chapters, it should take much less than one hour a day to be prepared for investment decisions and action. Furthermore, at least 50 percent of the time your money will never be invested in the option market, or in any other market. Only a consistent stock market loser can appreciate the effect this can have on one's sleeping habits.

Other forms of investments than the stock and option markets are available to the small investor with risk capital. Some examples are the bond market, mutual funds, art forms, coin collections, and commodity markets which deal all the way from gold bullion futures to options on pork bellies. The bond market is not really the Little Guy's game, while art treasures and coin collections have never caught my investment fancy. Equally uninteresting, in my opinion, are mutual funds, which have always impressed me as the best way to average losses over someone else's portfolio, rather than over a few inappropriate personal selections. But I suspect that, with the exception of commodity trading, a good many small investors rule out these forms of investment primarily because they lack the potential for large capital gains in a short period of time. Strangely enough, I believe the small investor displays his conservative side by steering clear of commodity markets, which he construes as a blatant form of gambling with high risks and all the investment quality of off-track betting. I further suspect that for some, if the truth were known, it's because the number of tips on the horses and stock market far exceed any "inside information" received on commodities. It also may be easier to relate to a Xerox copier than a bushel of soybeans.

Although many a small investor has a very conservative side, there is still a powerful yearning to hit the fabulous jackpot. Yet, in the stock market, these expectations have almost zero probability of occurring. Based on market averages and with perfect timing, studies show the stock market in the past decade or so would have provided at best a 15 percent annual return on investment. But who has perfect market timing? Certainly not the Little Guy. Hence, as so often is the case, expectations are drastically out of line with reality.

I see nothing wrong with the small investor hoping for and dreaming of the big market payoff. Without the hope of rising above the financial middle ground, the Little Guy is doomed to a life of perpetual averageness. If nothing else, the message of this book is that the Little Guy can win—and win big. It takes discipline, the courage to act decisively, and many times the patience not to act at all. In any event, it's essential to break the Little Guy tradition of being the perpetual underdog loser by adopting a new and better approach.

In chapter 8 a method of trading options is outlined that provides this new and perhaps radical approach. The trading guidelines and other recommendations set forth are generally contrary to the ordinary brand of investment advice to which the small investor is usually subjected. No play-it-safe broker would ever dream of mentioning such a revolutionary scheme, but then again it's usually the play-it-safe crowd who never advance beyond the vanilla stage. Meanwhile they rack up steady-as-you-go losses.

To participate in option trading as described in later chapters, the small investor should probably have a minimum of $4,000 to $5,000 in available risk capital. It's not mandatory, but highly desirable. This allows one to play for high stakes with some diversification and a chance to qualify for large, meaningful gains. But since no one has yet discovered a magic recipe for the coveted free lunch, one should be prepared to lose up to one-half of his invested capital, even if all the rules are followed. If the guidelines are disregarded, the whole bankroll can quickly vanish.

These qualifying statements are made, at least figuratively, for the benefit of widows and orphans. Risk capital means just what it says: there's risk involved! keep the grocery money in the cookie jar.

Not every small investor is emotionally suited to carry out the procedures set forth in the following chapters. If this is true for you, forget the strategy and save your money. However, if you really are the typical small investor, there is still likely to be some new information or market insight to be gained by reading on. It should more than offset the price of the book.

To fully appreciate the need and usefulness of my current approach to market investments, it's instructive to hear how I continually deceived myself while trying to conquer Wall Street in earlier days. Most likely, if you are or ever were a Little Guy, there will be plenty of occasion to identify with the silly, cumbersome, and irrational actions I faithfully followed. This road to financial disaster may be unpleasantly familiar.

2

The Formative Years

My very first stock market investment was made in 1960, shortly after moving to Los Angeles to work for the Ramo Wooldridge Corporation, a high-technology aerospace company. At the time, I was coming off a two-year term at the Massachusetts Institute of Technology as a post-doctoral mathematics instructor. I left with an abundance of confidence to take on the nonacademic world. Although I had all the qualifications of a computer scientist, I had absolutely zero preparation for the world of investments. But then, after all, how could picking stocks and making lots of money be all that difficult? Simple! Without even trying, I acted the part of the classic Little Guy and with more skill than I care to remember.

When I first set foot in a brokerage house to open an account, I had what I considered a full complement of investor knowledge, gleaned, of course, from a paperback primer on stock market operation. As I was directed to the daily *floor broker,* I'm sure he must have been rubbing his hands in anticipation of meeting Mr. Joe Loser for a morning séance. A floor broker is the guy who pulls the duty of welcoming walk-ons from the street. To rely on these people for financial advice is a great way to live dangerously.

After my account was opened, I left with several research reports from the free literature counter and subsequently selected two stocks for purchase. One was Fedders Corporation, which caught my attention because the price was low and the temperature outside in the San Fernando Valley was high. How could the stock of a company that made air conditioners not go through the roof? The second choice was Thiokol Chemical Corporation. In 1960 rocket engines were in and would certainly consume exorbitant quantities of propellant fuel. Both purchases were in odd lots, of course, so there would be no mistake that this was truly a Little Guy dabbling in the market. And how about the reasoning behind these decisions? Really deep thinking! About the only plus for these transactions was the accidental diversification. To make a long story short, both issues were closed out within a few months at a loss, not for valid reasons, you understand, but because I needed the money for other things. I entered the market like a Little Guy so why not leave like one?

Fortunately, my investment record immediately improved. My job became more demanding and for several years my interest in the market waned to the point where I closed my brokerage account and sat on the sidelines. It was not until four years later that I renewed my acquaintance with Wall Street.

In May of 1964 I joined Scientific Data Systems (SDS), a small, three-year-old computer manufacturer located in Santa Monica, California. The company was about to go public with its first equity offering. There was an air of excitement about the place that I had never experienced before, or for that matter, since. Almost all professional employees, including myself, had stock options that were exercisable in the future at what proved to be extremely low prices. When the offering was complete, the IRS must have gained at least a dozen new millionaires. Unfortunately, my relatively late arrival excluded me from this select group. Even so, the rapid price rise in SDS stock as trading increased brought home to me the extraordinary potential for financial gain that exists in the market. This experience at SDS probably also explains why to this day I have a lingering penchant for computer stocks. But it's also a classic example of how a Little Guy occasionally gets lucky and finds himself in a superb stock that serves him well. In 1969 SDS was acquired by Xerox Corporation, and in 1972, when I finally sold the last of my original SDS stock (by then XRX), the net capital gain was well over 1000 percent of my original investment. However, it was not until 1971 that I returned to the general stock market to reinstate my credentials as a Little Guy loser.

In 1966 I ventured into the entrepreneurial world by forming a computer programming company servicing the aerospace industry. The timing of this move was ideal because business conditions were good and getting better. Although the company never reached large proportions it remained profitable throughout my three-and-one-half-year tenure as president, and it provided me with an excellent opportunity to gain a firsthand knowledge of business fundamentals. This experience has generally proved beneficial as well as educational. But for a latent small investor, it also had one important drawback. Too much knowledge of business detail tends to make the Little Guy a fundamentalist in his investment decisions. That is, he tends to rely on and correlate published data on a company's status or future potential to arrive at market

decisions. It is self-delusion to think there is an orderly
logic that can be applied to achieve investment success.
Knowledge of a company's fundamentals is fine if it's used
as just one piece of the puzzle. Additionally, the pure
fundamentalist, by his very nature, is willing to wait for his
facts to ferment whereas the Little Guy I'm addressing
wants his payoff in the much shorter term.

As the 1970s were approaching, it became clear to me
that the aerospace industry was on the verge of trouble and
that with its arrival my company would be facing hard
times. This was the signal to surrender independence and
take shelter with a merger partner to wait out the storm.
After an on-again, off-again courtship the nuptials were
finally set. The acquisition timing in early 1970 was near
optimum. Shortly thereafter new aerospace activity came
to a standstill, and the industry led the nation into a severe
recession. However, this marriage, consummated on earth,
was definitely not made in heaven. The merger into a
larger New York software company proved a disaster, and
I was fortunate to recover my original investment. Within
a year the new parent company was on the brink of col-
lapse, and before long my business background was further
extended—this time with a short course on the fine points
of bankruptcy a la chapter 11.

The merger in 1970 was accomplished via an exchange
of stock, but as a principal in the transaction I was unable
to sell my newly acquired shares fast enough to keep pace
with their demise. In spite of this frustrating experience,
the Little Guy's spark of hope for making it big was
rekindled. Once again I was ready to submit myself to
bigger and better market losses.

3

Profile of a Busy Loser

As I emerged from the computer world in 1971, I made the fateful decision to confront Wall Street head-on. I set aside an initial stake of approximately $35,000 in cash and current stock holdings to pursue my heretofore elusive fortune. But no dabbling this time. I would treat this endeavor as a full-time business. It seemed reasonable that with hard work and diligent attention success would not be all that elusive. In no time at all I would be buying that lot on the corner of Easy Street and Uptick Avenue.

I conceived a plan of action and adopted a schedule of activities. One of my first undertakings was to rent space for an office and equip it with furniture, telephone, and TV. Every business needs an office, doesn't it? The TV was essential for a special reason. In Los Angeles, as in several other major cities, there's a financial station that transmits a blow-by-blow description of market action. It comes

complete with visual shots of the tote boards, which display
such current statistics as the Dow-Jones industrial averages, volume, figures, and other information on both the
New York and American exchanges. But most exciting of
all to the Little Guy are the continuously running tapes at
the bottom of the screen displaying price action, similar to
those prancing across the wall of your local brokerage
house. However, there's an additional mystique to these TV
tapes. They're purposely delayed by fifteen minutes so as
not to compete with the even greater thrill you can achieve
watching this exciting action while seated next to your local
broker. Oh, what a frustration to see the price of your
favorite stock passing by in ever changing increments and
knowing that, even if you call your broker immediately to
buy (or worse yet, to sell), you're already fifteen minutes
late.

It's probably worthwhile to summarize here my opinion
on the net effect of financial TV on the small investor, or
for that matter, on the boardroom loiterer, his social
counterpart. I suspect that the Little Guy has a difficult
time handling it. Emotions run high watching those statistics change right in front of your eyes and with every click
and clatter the boards seem to say, "It's your move!" But
reckless emotion is the last thing a Little Guy can afford.
Not taking any market action is almost always better than
an impulsive one.

My experience with financial TV also points up another
major problem. This medium seems to attract more than
its share of charlatans. They prey upon gullible viewers by
promoting not only their corporations, but other wares such
as market letters, investment counseling, books, coins,
seminars, or whatever. Some of these people can be the
worst kind of menace because they come across the tube as
highly sincere, self-confident, and knowledgeable. With the
Little Guy more than ready to grasp for any straw that will

change his luck, the kill is quick and easy. More than once I joined the crowd and lunged for the perfect answer, only to come away with the short straw. The only consolation I ever received for these escapades was that occasionally some form of underlying fraud was eventually discovered by the Securities and Exchange Commission and reported in the press. No action, mind you, just a polite reprimand. However, to have these people publicly exposed is hardly compensation for one's folly.

Before leaving the subject of financial TV I hasten to point out that the medium also has its obvious good points which tend to offset some of the potential evils. One of these advantages is the availability of closing market statistics, some of which are difficult to obtain from regular newspapers. Also, for those who like to keep informed with up-to-the-minute financial and world news, such TV stations are very informative. Occasionally you may even find a reasonably astute market analyst who can broaden your market insight. But actually, I'm sorry to say, the Little Guy is probably playing with fire when he continually bombards himself with financial news and commentary. There's such a temptation to think you're on top of things. And when you feel it's all starting to make sense, that's when you're in real trouble. Just keep an open mind and stick to the basic facts. Awareness is fine, but presumed knowledge can be downright hazardous to your financial health. The market will tell you what's taking place via its closing statistics. Although the majority of small part-time investors don't realize it, their daily preoccupation with making a living may be a great blessing in disguise.

In addition to setting up a functional office, I set out to increase my rather shallow knowledge of the stock market in preparation for the upcoming action. In this area I actually did a few things right. To begin with I read some of the classic books on stock market investing which gave

me an overall perspective. Some of these books were
obtained from the public library or borrowed from friends.
The bibliography contains a partial list of books from my
own relatively small investment library, all of which helped
formulate my early thinking. Not all of these books are
innately beneficial to the novice investor. For example,
Richard Ney's books, which imply some sort of conspiracy
between market specialists and other really big guys, tend
to provide more of a rationale for one's losses than a
positive and successful market approach, especially for the
small investor. But overall, the background reading proved
useful as a framework for the future.

In addition to general background information, every
stock market investor should have some familiarity with
technical analysis. For this purpose I selected a basic text
on the principles of charting which proved to be more than
adequate. In fact, for the market strategy I describe later
on, some elementary knowledge of technical analysis is not
only highly desirable, but indispensable. To apply my
newly acquired knowledge, I subscribed to the *Standard &
Poor's Monthly Stock Charts,* which can be updated on a
selective and daily basis. Again, this has proved to be one of
my more prudent moves.

For keeping abreast of current events and financial news,
I never failed to read the *Wall Street Journal* or *Barrons.*
For a somewhat broader outlook I subscribed to *U. S. News
& World Report* and *Business Week* which I literally read
from cover to cover. The electronics industry was singled
out for special consideration via the publications of *Elec-
tronic News* and *Computerworld.* All in all, I felt my
weekly ration of business news was more than sufficient,
and to this day I retain these same basic reading habits.

Early on, I discovered the *Trade Levels Report,* a most
valuable publication from Trade Levels, Inc., of Woodland
Hills, California. It contains a weekly summary of market

activity together with corresponding charts, indicators, and other reference material. I highly recommend it to any active investor. Unfortunately, the full importance and usefulness of this report escaped me for a number of years. At the present time I still receive it, together with its companion report on the option market. I make use of these data primarily for reinforcing my investment selections and market timing. Now for some of the unpleasant memories:

One of my most foolhardy attempts to masquerade as a sophisticated investor was subscribing to *Business Conditions Digest,* the Commerce Department's monthly publication of business indicators. The number and complexity of these monthly charts were absolutely mind boggling. I'm not even sure the Commerce Department knew what they all meant, but then maybe that's why they were for sale. Needless to say, I never renewed my original subscription.

By far the most dangerous publication I ever had the misfortune to order was the *Standard & Poor's Earnings Estimates.* It seems unreal that I would pay good money to have myself financially destroyed. Actually, a case can be made for self-destruction since I was naive enough to think these estimates would not only turn out to be accurate, but they could also be used as the basis for predicting price movements in the corresponding stocks. In retrospect, this is a classic example of how a Little Guy thinks he can outsmart the system if he only has the right combination of tools to work with. But as a general rule, information that is public knowledge is at best neutral in value for making investment decisions.

The world of stock market investments would be incomplete indeed without the numerous pundits who spread their divine revelations via the infamous market letter. Just as they were the experts, I became the grand master of the trial subscription. Confusion reigned! And when it became clear that there was no magical shortcut for finding the golden goose, I quickly befriended my local mailman by lightening his load.

Enough about market literature. Let's move on to stockbrokers. After my initial entry into the market, my next broker was recommended by a friend. Some friend! This broker had a "thing" for obscure, over-the-counter (OTC) stocks that only moved one way—South. Of course, after the initial recommendations the ultimate buy decisions were always my own. I never could fault the guy, however, for his sell recommendations, since none were ever forthcoming. This would only have crystallized my paper losses.

By the time I hit my stride as a seasoned loser, I had accumulated three different brokers whom I used concurrently. This tripled my velocity on the way to the poorhouse. When I include my own misadventures, the ride was even faster. I was into new issues, secondary offerings, and, it seems in retrospect, just about anything the brokers wanted to unload. My transactions were always on the long side and there wasn't a single day that I was out of the market. The situation couldn't even be summed up by the old saying easy come, easy go because the easy come part was certainly anything but easy. Looking back, it's even more frustrating to think that for a good portion of my losing streak I was operating in a bull market environment.

Most serious investors make use of well-established market indicators to guide them in their market decisions. Not me! I had to develop my own special set. With a few exceptions my personalized indicators provided little more than an opportunity to develop time-consuming charting habits. This busywork only served to reinforce my innate, all-American belief that hard work could be equated with success.

Complementing my external sources for gaining market insight and providing investment guidance, I also had to contend with my own ill-conceived reasoning and highly emotional behavior. The latter was more than evident in my regular, day-by-day market activities.

I typically began my daily schedule of baby-sitting the market by rising at 6:00 A.M. After the usual splashing of soap and water, I worked my way through the morning *Los Angeles Times* and a hasty breakfast. I always probed the front section of the paper for any late-breaking news that might affect the opening of the market at 7:00 A.M. This was then followed by a manhunt through the business section. I searched everywhere for any article that might disturb the stocks in my portfolio. More often than not, no news was equated with good news.

Next I set out to pick up the *Wall Street Journal* and proceed to my office. It was a two-block stretch, and the pace of my walk was generally geared to the stimulus I received from the early news. A fast step usually meant impending danger to my meager assets, and I knew the *Journal* could expand on, or diminish, my fears. When I reached my office I quickly scanned the summary articles on the front page for any additional events I might have missed and then read follow-up articles on important items. By 7:00 A.M., in either calm or panic, I had the TV on and began playing my role of financial tycoon. Actually it's better described as Archie Bunker in his finest hour.

When the early news was alarming or there was an adverse press release on one of my issues, I found myself fighting off a knee-jerk reaction to sell. Even before the market opened, I was on the phone to my broker, dialing and disconnecting, as I struggled to come to a firm sell or hold decision. In many cases fear won out but the discarded issue deserved a better fate. What better way was there to reward my lack of confidence than to have the stock make a U-turn later in the day and finish substantially higher?

There are at least two major faults embodied in these early-morning shenanigans; on average that's one every thirty minutes. First off, it's highly questionable that most overnight world or national news events are, by themselves, capable of having more than a transient effect on the market. In fact, these perturbations usually occur at the market opening and quickly dissipate, if and when they occur at all. Yet the unsophisticated investor executes his trade precisely during the period of reaction that he's trying to avoid. Clearly, some news events do cause major market responses, but it's not practical to base an investment strategy on reacting to them.

Press releases and other business articles fall in the category of yesterday's news. Only the Little Guy seems surprised when they finally appear in print.

A second objection to this morning routine relates to intraday timing. As a general rule, I've found the market opening to be the worst time of day for making any transaction. This holds equally well for executions made with a market order or a limit order. From personal observation, the market often seems to move with a predictable daily rhythm. After the first sixty or ninety minutes, the early price momentum subsides and may even change direction to price levels beyond those at the opening. Then, during the middle third of the market day, there's generally a period of drifting price action while the New York boys call time-out for refreshments. Finally, the last sixty or ninety minutes of trading are characterized by more of the same early-morning action. Other patterns of daily market behavior also occur, but the one described above seems most common. Based on such a pattern of price action, the best time for any transaction is midday, whether the execution is a buy or a sell. So at the present time I avoid taking any kind of market action at the opening and grab the extra shut-eye instead.

If there's anything worse than reacting emotionally to news events, it's anticipating them and the type of market action they're going to produce. Nevertheless, this was an integral part of my daily operation. One of the best examples that comes to mind from my own repertoire is waiting for some major industrial strike to end. Most Little Guys, including myself, would interpret this as good news. But when the settlement is announced, what actually happens to the market? Take your pick. Anything can happen, including nothing. And when your guess is wrong, the latter is generally the best alternative you can hope for.

But that's only a small part of the total problem. It's during the waiting period before the event takes place that rational thinking becomes distorted and your assets are in greatest danger. It seems that, no matter how far down the market drops, and your own portfolio as well, there's a tendency to hold out for that offsetting rally that will bring you back to even. Good judgment is replaced by expectation, and the lower the prices go, the bigger the rally one must visualize. When it finally becomes clear that the two are totally out of line and still diverging, it's frustration time. Then, when the event ultimately does occur, it's only a question of totaling up the losses. And that's with, or without, an ensuing rally.

To make sure I didn't miss any special event that would affect the market, I maintained a time chart on which I recorded upcoming activities. These included presidential addresses, peace conferences, strike deadlines, new product announcements, earnings report dates, and so forth. In retrospect, however, I can't recall a single incident where this foolish busywork ever paid off. But on the other side of the ledger, it cost me dearly in lost points to the downside.

During this period I always maintained accurate and complete records of my investment results. On a daily basis I knew exactly the amount of my accumulated losses; there was little to record in the way of gains. I suspect now, however, that my approach to record keeping was the only businesslike aspect of all my investment undertakings.

By early 1973 my initial stake of $35,000 had dwindled to $15,000. And this result included the relatively large long-term capital gain I had in Xerox, mentioned earlier. An analysis of my transactions would indicate to any knowledgeable observer that the final results were almost inevitable. My records showed a large number of small purchases involving from 100 to 300 shares of moderately priced and low-volatile stocks. At any given time my portfolio usually contained from four to eight such issues. With this relatively small potential for achieving even a single large capital gain, there was absolutely no hope of making any significant amount of money except possibly in the very long term. But it certainly wasn't in my Little Guy nature to stay with someone else's recommendation when the big jackpot didn't arrive on my schedule.

In a final effort to lower the last lifeboat of my sinking ship, I opened a new account in my own neighborhood to make a final stand on home ground and in so doing bid farewell to my other brokers. This time it would be different. Any mistakes from here on in would be entirely my own. My new broker was given explicit instructions: "No recommendations! No phone calls! Just execute my market orders and, hopefully, don't botch up the instruction." What could be simpler—and coming from a walk-in no less?

Although my Little Guy thinking still precluded any immediate success, I have never regretted this impersonal form of broker-client relationship. To this day I consider broker recommendations, at best, a waste of time and at their worst, well, buyer beware.

By mid-1973 I was still floundering in search of that super stock that would change my destiny. With only $11,000 left of my original equity capital, I faced up to the reality of investment failure and, after shutting down my office, I returned to the world of computer applications instead of remaining in the fascinating arena of computer investments.

4

The Las Vegas Connection

There is an underlying pattern to the motivations and instincts of the small investor that transcends many aspects of his daily life. This is particularly true for those of us who were reared with the strong work ethic so pervasive on the American scene until the 1950s. Starting with this decade it seemed that the American dollar, once a symbol of personal pride in financial accomplishment, had subsequently been relegated to a position of scorn as the "almighty dollar."

But for many a Little Guy who's taken his share of knocks in the battle of paycheck stretching, the resulting scars are manifested by an ultraconservative financial attitude. Although it's difficult to fault this protective shield, such conservatism is frequently deceptive. That is, too much conservatism is not conservative at all. Perhaps more unfortunate is the resulting inability to ever achieve extraordinary financial gains, much less financial independence.

The financial conservatism of the small investor and his associated Little Guy thinking are perhaps best illustrated by his approach to gambling. After a number of visits to the gambling casinos in Las Vegas, I find it possible to draw some interesting parallels. There seems to be a remarkable similarity between Little Guy instincts for both gambling and investing. For the most part I can speak of this connection from personal experience. Any identification you make with the analogies will remain your secret.

It seems highly likely to me that anyone who can spend hour after hour playing a slot machine might well also own a portfolio of stocks characterized by low prices, low trading volume, and most likely odd lots. In either case, money management is purely mechanical. No thinking allowed! With average luck the slot jockey can stretch a twenty dollar bill into several hours of anticipation and a sore elbow. The thrill of a five dollar jackpot must be every bit as exciting, and probably as infrequent, as having one of his portfolio dogs make the most active list. This kind of action is a great time killer in Las Vegas. It has a certain fascination about it and, perhaps, some redeeming social value. But its counterpart in the investment world is downright inexcusable. Moreover, because of its somewhat poorer liquidity, it even rates below the proverbial mattress as a suitable place to put money. About the best that can be said for both parts of this analogy is that it's usually difficult to lose large sums while continually playing against odds that would make even Jimmy the Greek cringe. But the downside protection afforded by low stakes and slow erosion of assets should never be construed as conservative, at least not in the overall spectrum of investments. The fact that low-priced stocks are bought and then stashed away, only to be resurrected later for a formal burial, is anything but conservative.

The majority of serious gamblers do not rely on a spinning wheel or any other mechanical device to achieve success. This type prefers to rely on personal skill to tip the odds of winning in his favor. He insists that his fortune not be won or lost on the basis of the complicated laws of physics which decide the relative positions of three cherries or the particular crack in a revolving disc that will trap a bouncing ball. Among the several outlets that satisfy this requirement in Las Vegas is the blackjack table. Its green welcome mat particularly invites the weary gambler to take the load off his feet while it removes the load from his wallet.

Without belaboring the rules of playing blackjack, suffice it to say that the house dealer plays against his guests in a one-on-one fashion. Each guest is attempting to come closest to the sum of twenty-one by receiving a sequence of two or more cards. High cards count as ten, the ace is optionally eleven or one. The odds in this game favor the house because the dealer always plays last and wins on all ties. Various strategies have been devised to allow players to not only narrow the odds but in some cases to actually reverse them. The latter strategies border on computer applications and when executed manually certainly must take the fun out of gambling. For the most part the casinos have applied countermeasures to bring the odds back in their favor. But the point to be made here is that the blackjack player can definitely increase his odds of winning by preparing an optimum strategy and then concentrating on applying it.

This general category of gambler is related to the group of serious investors that includes both Big and Little Guys. Investors in this category may also be in the overall majority. However, the representative Little Guy both

gambles and invests with no set goals. Although he has
confidence in his ability to win, and comes prepared with
adequate strategy, he doesn't fully appreciate the odds
against him. He decreases the size of his bets when he's
winning and then keeps on playing with house money. How
could this money possibly be his own, since he didn't earn
it? In the stock market he averages down with his
purchases when prices are dropping to smooth out his losses
and his basically conservative nature prevents him from
pyramiding up when the market is rising. Without definite
objectives it's only a matter of time before Ms. Lady Luck
becomes the house madam. When frustration is finally
rampant, all semblance of a strategy is usually abandoned
and silly irrational actions become the order of the day. Of
course, not all small investors are losers at blackjack, but
the exceptions are sufficiently rare as to make a winning
profile difficult.

The final gambling analogy to be made here is of particular importance because it's related to the investment
approach recommended in this book. It also involves one of
the most exciting of all games of chance. It's affectionately
called craps, no doubt after a loser's famous last words. The
action can be just about as fast and wild as one can throw a
pair of dice and yell, "Baby needs new shoes," or some
other profound statement.

The game of dice, or crap shooting, is not as sim-
pleminded as it may appear to the casual observer.
Without delving into all the rules and ramifications of the
game there are betting procedures (e.g., taking the odds on
each roll) that if followed, allow the player to bring his
odds of winning into very close parity with the house odds.
Of course, the casinos always retain a winning edge, but the
crap game properly played offers the best basic gambling
opportunity in Las Vegas when playing against the house.
The only exception to this statement that I'm aware of

involves some of the previously mentioned blackjack strategies which, for all practical purposes, have been outlawed.

The Little Guy who plays craps is seldom a serious candidate for coming away a big winner because taking the odds and betting on each roll can quickly escalate into a large dollar amount in total wagers. Notwithstanding the improved odds, it goes against the Little Guy's conservative nature to realize that a single roll of the dice can wipe out so many bets. Yet it's precisely this ability to leverage successive bets, and simultaneously take advantage of any winning momentum, that distinguishes the successful player from the loser. One good hot streak with the dice can more than offset a prolonged series of one-shot wagers.

A crap table in Las Vegas with heavy winners is not difficult to spot. There's usually excessive noise and people pressing in two and three deep, to belly up to the table. It's like a miniature football stadium with the home team scoring at will to a standing-room-only crowd. You can almost feel the electricity and excitement as the croupier calls out, "Ee O Leven! A Winner! Pay the line!" There's no mistake about it. This is a winning table, and the time for action is now.

In addition to recognizing a winning table and playing it to the hilt, it's equally important for the successful crap shooter to sense when the action is winding down. When the second and third teams take to the field the gambling pro heads for the exit. Why bet on another touchdown when the yardage is coming tough? The winner picks up his chips, eases on down the road, and comes back another time.

I personally like the analogy of crap shooting with investing in the options market. I don't say this in any reckless or derogatory way. On the contrary, I see the options market as the only feasible outlet for the small investor to achieve any large financial gains. And with proper selection and execution, as explained in later chapters, these gains can be obtained without undue risk of heavy losses in investment capital. Moreover, as in playing craps, the rewards can be large and made within a short period of time.

Although the signs may not be quite as dramatic as in spotting a winning crap table, the small investor must learn when to enter the option market. The exit process is partially solved by the expiration feature of options. But like the crap shooter who protects his gains, it's also important to detect when the upward momentum and potential for success are deteriorating in a given option. If one can master these decisions with a minimum of emotion, the option market is the Little Guy's best hope for attaining superior financial success.

5

The Newest Game in Town

This chapter contains a brief discussion of the listed options market for the benefit of those readers unfamiliar with its essential features and potential as an investment tool. A total stranger to options may find the presentation much too concise and prefer a more extensive introduction to the subject matter. A number of publications are available for this purpose, and they can usually be obtained free of charge from your regular broker. On the other hand, the experienced options trader may wish to skip the following material; he may proceed directly to the next chapter without any loss of continuity.

There are basically two different types of stock option—the *call* option and its reverse counterpart the *put* option. When a single call option is sold on a given stock it allows the buyer to purchase 100 shares of this stock at a specified price throughout a fixed period of time. The put option is defined as in the previous sentence with the word *purchase* replaced by *sell*. The price specified in the option is called the exercise or strike price, and if the stock is never purchased, in the case of a call option (or never sold with a put), the option is said to have expired. Otherwise the option is *exercised* and the buyer *calls* for the underlying stock to be delivered to him. When a put option is exercised, the option holder puts his underlying stock to the option seller and collects the exercise price.

One of the most important advantages associated with stock options as an investment tool is the increased leverage they provide. Frequently even a small price move in the underlying stock results in a large percentage change in the option. This exciting feature must be tempered, of course, by the knowledge that such price swings can work both ways. At the same time, the small investor can often amplify this leverage even further by working with high-priced stocks indirectly through options. Although options are not marginable, their relative cost is usually much lower than the price of the underlying stock.

Options on most actively traded stocks have been available to buyers for decades via a form of over-the-counter (OTC) market. The exercise price was usually set at the current market price and the option period was typically either three, six, or nine months. The purchase price of such an option is called its premium. This is the price the buyer is willing to pay above the intrinsic value of the option. In these early cases the intrinsic value was zero since the current stock price and the exercise price of the option were equal. In general, whenever the exercise price is greater than or equal to the current stock price, the intrinsic value of a call option is zero and the option is said to be *out of the money*. Conversely, when the current price is greater than the exercise price the option is *in the money*.

Buying options in the OTC market was relatively simple, but selling was a different matter. There were numerous expiration dates and a wide range of exercise prices among the outstanding options. This meant that, for all practical purposes, the original market makers were the only potential buyers in a rather makeshift secondary options market. Resale prices, if available at all, were less than optimum. This resulted in a minimum of liquidity on the sell side, and hence options usually were either exercised or expired worthless. This lack of flexibility made the purchase of options a questionable form of investment at best.

In April of 1973 all this changed with the opening of the Chicago Board Options Exchange (CBOE). For the first time, call options were traded on this exchange in a controlled environment much like that for stocks. Expiration dates were standardized, and exercise prices were confined to convenient values that varied in multiples of five or ten points. Perhaps most important, the CBOE market makers provided the basic liquidity that removed the previous either/or alternative associated with closing out options.

After the initial success of the CBOE was established, call options began trading on a number of other exchanges. At the present time over 1,500 options are traded on more than 200 underlying stocks on the American, Philadelphia, Midwest, and Pacific exchanges as well as on the CBOE. A few options have listings on more than one exchange to allow for greater competition, and options on additional stocks are periodically added to the overall list. A list of optionable stocks is presented immediately after the bibliography.

It's difficult for the outsider to distinguish between the mechanical execution of trades on the various option exchanges. Theoretically the CBOE operates with market makers, whereas the others retain the specialist system ordinarily associated with listed stocks. About the only

worthwhile advice that can be given to anyone contemplating an option trade is the same that applies to stock transactions. If you really want an execution, always do it at the
prevailing bid or asked price. Usually it's the Little Guy
trying to save an eighth or a quarter of a point who ends up
turning his economy-size thinking into a king-size loss of
either money or opportunity.

The converse of buying an option is writing or selling
one. When the option writer actually owns the underlying
stock it's called a *covered write*. If not, it's called a *naked
write* to emphasize the added exposure of being called to
deliver the stock. The naked option writer is similar to the
short seller in the stock market although perhaps a bit more
adventuresome because of the high leverage. The number
of outstanding options on a given stock with the same
characteristics (e.g., exercise price) is called the *open interest*. The daily volume of options trading can be found in
the transaction tables of the *Wall Street Journal*. When
trading near-term options, with only a few months left
before expiration, it can be important to deal only in
actively traded options with a fairly high open interest.
These conditions are necessary ingredients for maximum
liquidity.

When an option is selling for less than fifty cents and is
more than five points out of the money, trading is confined
only to closing transactions. During these periods the open
interest cannot increase and the option is said to be
restricted. These situations usually arise when the option is
far out of the money and the expiration date is near. When
an option is restricted all speculation is suspended.

In some respects the options markets suffer from the
same secretive image associated with the stock market. For
example, it's nearly impossible for a Little Guy to find out
how many naked writes are out on a given option, much
less those that have been written by specialists or market

makers. But then again, if this information were published, I'm sure the small investor would find some ingenious way to use it to his detriment.

Stock options are identified by symbols consisting of three to five characters. The last two characters always specify the expiration month and exercise price, while the initial characters are the usual code letters for the underlying stock. For example, the symbol XRXJN represents the Xerox October 70 option. It's actually the relative position of both *J* and *N* in the alphabet that decode into October 70. The entire set of coded relationships appears in table 1. Only the month need be specified since the last day an option may be traded is the third Friday of its expiration month. Options formally expire on the next day (Saturday). However, unless you're going to exercise an option, the prudent Little Guy should probably close out any position at least by early morning of the last trading day.

It is important to remember that there is no guarantee that any position can be closed, regardless of how actively the option is traded or how large its open interest. Each sell order must always be matched on an exchange with a corresponding buy order. Therefore, when more than a small number of options is involved, it may be prudent to initiate closing transactions on portions of one's total position well in advance of the last trading day.

Although option trading as discussed in later chapters does not involve the exercise of options, there are firm time limits when an exercise notice must be conveyed to your broker for execution. Rules regarding such notice, as well as the mechanics involved, are spelled out in *Prospectus: The Options Clearing Corporation.* This document is not only made available from your broker, but every options trader is required to sign a statement to the effect that he has read and understands its contents. It is must reading and deserves more than the traditional once-over-lightly.

On the listed options exchanges each issue with fixed exercise price has three expiration months for which options are traded concurrently. A three-month period separates the expiration dates, and as each date passes, a new set of options becomes available for trading. At the present time most options expire in the months of January, April, July, and October and are referred to as the *January series* of options. February and March series are defined in an analogous manner.

From a tax point of view, stock options are a capital asset. The result of buying and subsequently selling an option is treated as either a long-term or a short-term capital gain, depending on how long the option was held. However, the Tax Reform Act of 1976 extended the holding period for long-term capital gains, and as a result long-term considerations do not apply to the listed option market.

The settlement date for an option trade is the next trading day following the transaction. For tax purposes, a loss can be claimed as of the trading date, and a gain is recorded on the settlement date.

Like the unwarranted concern over high commission fees, tax considerations should seldom, if ever, enter into the Little Guy's investment decisions. On second thought, strike "seldom" and make that "never enter into consideration." If any trade is questionable on either of these two counts the decision is almost always clear. If the trade is a potential buy, then forget it; if it's a sell, proceed to unload posthaste.

The CBOE provides a summary of overall tax implications associated with options in a pamphlet titled *Tax Considerations in Using CBOE Options.* It may be obtained through your local brokerage house or by writing

Expiration Month	Letter of Alphabet	Exercise Prices		
JAN.............	A	$ 5	$105	$205
FEB	B	10	110	210
MARCH.........	C	15	115	215
APRIL	D	20	120	220
MAY............	E	25	125	225
JUNE	F	30	130	230
JULY	G	35	135	235
AUG	H	40	140	240
SEPT............	I	45	145	245
OCT	J	50	150	250
NOV	K	55	155	255
DEC	L	60	160	260
	M	65	165	265
	N	70	170	270
	O	75	175	275
	P	80	180	280
	Q	85	185	285
	R	90	190	290
	S	95	195	295
	T	100	200	300

Table 1. Options Symbol Codes

directly to CBOE, Inc., LaSalle at Jackson, Chicago, Illinois 60604. An interesting opinion, worthy of note, is expressed in this summary regarding the so-called Wash Sale Rule. According to this provision of the Internal Revenue Code, a loss on the sale of a security is deferred if the seller reacquires the security within a thirty-day period on either side of the sell transaction. Assuming an option is a security for tax purposes, the opinion expressed is that the rule may well apply for the sale and repurchase of an option with the same expiration date and exercise price.

But when either of the latter two conditions is different, the Wash Sale Rule does not apply.

As a final remark on trading call options, it should be noted that, as with the stock market, stop loss orders and limit orders for downside protection are also available. However, on certain exchanges, limit orders are accepted only on a not-held basis. This means the execution of a limit order is not guaranteed, and one should check with his broker for specifics on any particular transaction. The options trader may also specify that an option be sold when the underlying stock drops to a prescribed value.

Put options began trading on a number of option exchanges in 1977. However, they were not available at the time my options trading strategy was developed. The implication of course is that currently there are even more options strategies to consider, some involving the combined use of puts and calls. Nevertheless, I personally am more anxious to adopt and apply the approach outlined in chapter 8 to bear market environments using puts instead of calls. More about this possibility appears in chapter 11.

6

Shifting Sentiment

In August 1976 it was announced that the Securities and Exchange Commission (SEC) was beginning a study of why stock options have more attraction than equity securities for many investors. The commission was allegedly concerned that option trading was drawing off investor funds that otherwise might be going to small companies in need of speculative capital. But it seems to me that undertaking such a study was either exceptionally naive, or worse yet, ludicrous. As a small investor I have my own theory on the subject.

I personally tend to classify stock market investors into three groups based on the extent of their interest and involvement. At one end of the spectrum is the grossest Little Guy. In Las Vegas he heads directly for the slot machines. In the market he dabbles in offbeat stocks and can't recognize a winner because he's never met one. He usually buys on a recommendation, often with the most fragile supporting rationale, whether the source be his barber or his broker. Investments are almost always oriented toward the long term, and he rarely strays beyond the purchase of stocks. After accumulating a portfolio of special situations, he then plays the faithful shepherd waiting for his initial judgment and patience to be not only justified, but handsomely rewarded. These Little Guys are the ones who buy and hold stock in all those third and fourth tier companies that numerically constitute the bulk of corporate America. These are also the issues that professionals never give more than a passing glance to as they scan down the newspaper stock quotations to find their select group of personal favorites. With a few exceptions there's not even a nodding acquaintance with stocks off the New York Stock Exchange. This leaves it open for the Little Guy to pick and choose from among a cemetery of once active and promising issues. About the most charitable comment that can be made on such behavior is that the small investor in this category serves a patriotic function by providing at least a minimum degree of liquidity for the American system of capitalism. But, all in all, it's a thankless and, for the most part, unrewarding role.

Generally this set of unsophisticated investors is an uncomplaining lot, at least publicly. They tend to attribute their lack of success to their own bad luck or shortcomings rather than to faulty outside advice or the mysterious inner workings of the market system itself. Losses simply aren't discussed, and when they are eventually taken, it's only with reluctance. Nevertheless, the inevitable back-and-forth trading that takes place in these secondary issues, as they pass from one Little Guy to another, provides a floor under commission revenue for the brokerage community. These bread-and-butter transactions prop up the industry with a minimum of aggravation and effort.

A second category of stock market investor represents the opposite extreme and includes all the professional money people who derive a major portion of their livelihood from the market. This includes not only those who observe from afar and confine their activity solely to investing and trading, but others who are part of the operational system, such as specialists and exchange members. A common denominator shared among those in this category is that they all have a large financial stake riding on market investments. This qualifies them for membership in what's often called the inner circle where the perspective of the market is altogether different from that of the Little Guy. For these fraternity brothers it's a highly desirable place to do business while passing the time of day. Their financial clout practically guarantees success, except occasionally when some act of God intervenes to cause a temporary setback. But, all in all, this crowd, like the previous group, rarely complains. The difference is that they seldom have reason to be disgruntled. Still, it's all part of the market system, and, like it or not, the Little Guy must learn to accept this arena of combat if he's going to compete, no matter how unfair it may appear.

The majority of investors fall in a third category that lies between the previous two extremes. Most of these investors find the stock market a serious challenge and respect it as a formidable adversary in their attempts to supplement regular income with capital gains. There is a concerted effort by many to constantly improve their performance by making use of all available market data to piece together a successful plan of action. While a few succeed in achieving above-average gains, most find themselves the recipients of persistent losses.

Close examination of available data soon reveals the unequalness of the information flow within and outside the market system. Certain data are simply unavailable or else not presented in a timely manner. As a result there is an element of apparent secrecy that fosters the underlying suspicion of an unfair advantage deliberately preserved for professionals. This impression is further aggravated, if not completely set in concrete, when fraudulent practices detected among exchange members are treated by the SEC more like mischievous pranks than criminal activity. And these same statements hold for the host of other unsavory characters who operate on the market periphery.

But actually there's a much deeper and more tragic side to the whole situation that both government and market officials either fail to recognize or choose to ignore. Namely, the facts behind the fairness of market operation, or any practical role the SEC can play in regulating and policing such activity, are almost entirely immaterial for maintaining a viable, free market system. Of much more importance is the outward perception of even-handedness among all investors regardless of whether or not it actually exists. Unfortunately, I believe the current perception does not bode well for the securities industry.

I suspect a majority of small investors have very little to show in the way of capital gains for their overall efforts in the stock market. There are a number of reasons to support this conclusion, some of which have already been mentioned. But again, the cause may be less important than the effect. An irreversible disillusionment with the entire stock market system may have developed or already be well underway. The nagging frustration that accompanies continual financial losses is disturbing to any investor. When this frustration is coupled with doubts regarding the fairness of competition, the recent exodus from stock ownership should not be surprising.

The shift of investor interest away from the stock market has a foundation built on the reasons discussed above. But why turn to stock options instead of some other form of investment? For the most part, I firmly believe the answer is embodied in the discussions in chapter 1. There is an unfulfilled need to rise above financial uncertainty and attain more than life's basic necessities. To accomplish this, one must turn to more aggressive investments that are not limited in their potential for large gains. The option market provides just such an opportunity, notwithstanding the greater risks involved. Hence, when the SEC completes its study of options as an alternative to the stock market, I do not expect much in the way of surprises.

7

The Inevitable Recall to Active Duty

Starting in July 1973, I worked fifteen months on two back-to-back consulting assignments. This change of routine was actually a welcome relief from my previous lifestyle which involved a constant preoccupation with the stock market. During this period my withdrawal pains were relatively minor, and with a single exception it was cold turkey all the way. This isolated instance occurred shortly after the Arab oil embargo when my Little Guy instincts were just too overpowering to resist. I bought 500 shares of a tantalizing OTC number called KMS Industries at 5 1/2 per share. The company was into research on nuclear fusion, the fuel of the future. Unfortunately I proved to be one of the fools of the present. When I finally sold off my shares two and one-half years later, the Arabs were still pumping oil, and I had over a four-point loss to show for my clairvoyance.

In November 1974, having completed my consulting assignment, I again found myself preparing for an assault on Wall Street. Over the previous fifteen months the Dow-Jones industrial average had dropped from the 997 level to below 575. Contemplating this dramatic move left me simultaneously humble and optimistic. It was terrifying to think of what this decline would have done to my remaining assets had I continued to be an active participant in this downward slide. Who needed fifteen months? I surely would have been stripped clean much earlier, probably about the time the Dow Jones was zipping through 900.

Nevertheless I felt there was reason for optimism. Sometimes even a Little Guy can sense when enough is enough. But, for whatever my reasons, I concluded the bear market bottom had arrived and started to track and screen some of my favorite issues for buy candidates.

By early January 1975, in addition to KMS Industries, I held modest positions in three other stocks: Automatic Data Processing (AUD), Control Data Corporation (CDA), and MGIC Investment (MGI). I also bought my first listed option on the CBOE. This was a single Xerox July 60 option; not a big deal in option trading but more than sufficient to drive home a valuable message later on.

Those who follow the stock market will recall that the timing of these purchases was very near optimal since the bear market bottom of 570 on the Dow-Jones industrial average occurred on December 6, 1974. By the end of January 1975 my initial stock investment of $14,050 had grown to $18,225, an increase of nearly 30 percent. At the same time, however, my single Xerox option appreciated by over sixty-nine percent from $740 to $1,250. It was reassuring to know that my market judgment had proved correct, but at that point I would have been elated to find that it was merely a simple change of luck. What actually occurred was that I was swept up in the traditional year-end rally that just happened to coincide with the beginning of a new bull market.

Throughout the month of February I retained the same stock positions while adding four additional Xerox July 70 options. Before the month was out I sold all my options for an additional 12 percent gain while my total portfolio assets further increased by over 20 percent. On a relative month-to-month comparison, however, it was becoming clear that the initial surge of prices was slowing down, at least for my particular portfolio. It's at this point that the caution flag would have been raised for the successful investor. But I was still riding high, so why be concerned?

Early in February I began a new consulting assignment that would last over nine months. With the renewal of a regular income and two months of market victories under my belt, it was easy to forget my humiliating losses of a few years earlier. On one February day alone, my rather small market investment increased by over $2,800. It's no wonder I lost all fear of the marketplace after projecting my annual gain on this basis. Soon it would be, "Goodbye Redondo Beach; hello Beverly Hills."

Along with my delusions of grandeur, I was able to come away from this rewarding period with some very valuable insight. The high leverage and dramatic potential for gain associated with option trading left a lasting impression.

Suddenly, after the first week in March everything started to unravel. It was as if someone turned back the clock two years as I started to replay every Little Guy mistake I had ever made. I sold my AUD stock at 43 in early March only to see it hit 65 by July. Conversely I held my CDA and MGI while they came full circle and retraced all of their previous gains. Remembering my initial success, I also periodically continued to buy options on such underlying issues as Upjohn, Xerox, Tiger International, and Delta Airlines. My selection process was not only shallow and cavalier, but I used the oldest market timing tool of all—the hunch. In most cases I rode these kamikaze street-cars to the end of the line where the options literally expired. This Wall Street nightmare finally ended in October of 1975 when my early gains of $9,000 had deteri-orated into a net loss of equal amount.

In September of 1975, however, an incident occurred that was eventually to change my entire outlook on the market. More precisely, this event was to consolidate into a single investment approach all the features of a successful market strategy that I had only encountered before as isolated ingredients in separate transactions. As so often is the case, it all came about quite accidentally.

During a chance exposure to a market analyst on financial television, an interesting option strategy was presented. The strategy called for selling far-out-of-the-money, near-term options; i.e. options with only a month or two left before expiration and with at least a 10 or 15 percent spread between the current price and exercise price. To avoid extremely small premiums the options would be written on rather highly volatile issues and with as much diversification as possible. (In chapter 5 it's noted that there is a restriction on the sale of new options that are more than five points out of the money and with premiums less than fifty cents.) The reasoning behind this strategy is that very few stocks ever move 10 or 15 percent in such short periods of time, and the entire option premium would be a gain on expiration. But just in case the market refused to cooperate, the seller would buy back his position when the wayward option, say, doubled in price. If this all sounds too good to be true, don't run out and mortgage the house, at least not before you read on.

As much as I dislike hypothetical portfolios and make-believe trading, I set out to test this strategy. I selected eight October options that satisfied the basic requirements.

The underlying stocks were Alcoa, Avon, Citicorp, Halliburton, IBM, McDonald's, Texas Instruments, and Digital Equipment. By tracking the option prices from September 12 on, I got some interesting results. The options on Avon, IBM, McDonald's, Texas Instruments, and Digital Equipment, which expired on October 24, all would have been repurchased by early October since the options more than doubled in price during this period. Five out of eight were losers. But it was a small sample, and I did try it only once, so maybe it was just my magic touch striking again, having confused make-believe with reality.

Although the overall results could be rationalized away, there was one fascinating aspect of the experiment that captured my full attention. By October 23 the IBM OCT 200 option had gone from $1^{11}/_{16}$ to $15^{3}/_{8}$, while the Digital Equipment (DEC) OCT 120 moved from $2^{1}/_{8}$ to $14^{7}/_{8}$. These are percentage gains of 900 percent and 700 percent respectively which occurred in less than six weeks. Such numbers can hardly go unnoticed.

At this point it was not at all clear to me what had produced these remarkable results because the market in general experienced no more than a 6 percent increase while moving in an overall trading range. In my search for answers several possibilities came to mind. It could have been that IBM and DEC, as computer stocks, were both in a strong industry group. There was also the fact that both companies are perennial institutional favorites and, with the third quarter ending on September 30, there could have been major portfolio adjustments that benefited the issues. Additionally, some of the upside action might have been in anticipation of favorable quarterly earnings reports which were expected to be released in October. I suspect now, however, that the real answer embodied not only the net sum of these factors, but a number of others that no one mortal could hope to digest.

With renewed enthusiasm I started to formulate my new investment approach. It would be a positive strategy initially taking advantage of the remaining life in the current bull market. In some respects it would be exactly the reverse of the approach that I tested on paper. Yet in many ways it would retain both built-in safeguards and contingency plans for providing downside protection. The investment strategy that emerged is presented in the next chapter. It has been refined somewhat from its original conception as a result of subsequent application in the real market. Some personal experiences with its use are related in chapter 10.

8

Guidelines for Trading Options

This chapter describes the investment approach that developed out of my overall experience with trading options and my years of frustration in the stock market. It certainly doesn't carry any warranty on success, and it's not based on decades of market research or history. Nor has it passed the scrutiny of time as a revered and viable investment alternative. So why read on? Well, the only practical yardstick for measuring the success of this or any other market strategy is whether or not it actually works, here and now, regardless of any long-term track record.

Investment strategies based on years of statistical data and/or complicated technical analysis more often than not miss the mark. Engineer friends of mine have remarked on occasion about the possibility of applying Kalman Filter Theory (or whatever) to the movement of stock prices. I'm not even sure who or what Kalman is, but I do know that anything based on such a complicated-sounding scientific phrase would have to be worth at least a couple of grand in premeditated losses. If there's one thing you can count on, it's that the market doesn't have a degree in science and probably never will.

It's important for the Little Guy to adopt simple, easy-to-apply procedures for making his market decisions. Otherwise there may be no real understanding of the decision process. This in turn can lead one to conveniently, and perhaps subconsciously, shift the burden for success onto some complicated theory, when the ultimate responsibility for failure must rest on oneself. That doesn't mean one should act willy-nilly, but when the small investor depends on overly complex analysis to forecast either the market or individual price action, he's implicitly assuming a market predictability that rarely exists, except occasionally in the long term. It seems to me a more practical approach is to act only when the odds of success are highly favorable. And then, one should be prepared to run for cover just as soon as it becomes clear that the anticipated price movement is not about to materialize. Especially when trading near-term options, the lack of any price movement in the underlying stock can be nearly as devastating as movement in the wrong direction.

But let us get on with defining the proposed strategy by first presenting a set of option-trading guidelines. The strategy consists of *buying near-term, far-out-of-the-money call options in positive market environments. The underlying stocks should be actively traded, volatile issues in favorable industry groups.* There it is in two sentences; easy to state though somewhat difficult to come up with the combination of circumstances that satisfy all the criteria. In the remainder of this chapter these brief guidelines will be discussed in the context of a comprehensive approach to trading options with maximum leverage. The next chapter will concern itself with some special timing tools and other indicators that can be used in practical application.

It's been said that the overall success of any stock purchase can be attributed to three factors: (1) the general market environment (50 percent), (2) the popularity or favor of the industry group containing the stock (30 percent), and (3) the fundamental and technical condition of the stock itself (20 percent). A rigorous justification for this statement may or may not exist, but my personal experience in the market would attest to its general validity. Addressing the first part, I believe most everyone would agree that it's difficult enough for the small investor to make money in the best of markets, much less when the environment is neutral or bearish. So for trading on the long side, why diminish the odds of success still further by trying to operate under bear market conditions? Stick with the bulls and you may get nudged along with the crowd.

Fortunately, the ability to characterize the market environment is not all that difficult except in the short term. Once there's a perceptible change in the long-term market direction, either up or down, the normal business cycle generally unfolds in a more or less orderly fashion. It's with this long-term pattern that market history is most reliable. Although the length of such periods is variable, they're usually measured in years, and there are more than ample business indicators to signal their end. In any case, in the midst of a bull market cycle the situation is usually so obvious that almost every market commentator, analyst, and broker is bubbling with optimism. During bear market conditions the total euphoria slips a few percentage points, but the change is quite perceptible.

An intermediate-term period for the market is usually defined as lasting from three to six months, and various market indicators are available for determining when these minor cycles begin and end. Furthermore, when the market direction is reasonably well defined, these indicators are often remarkably accurate. It's a sideways market that can cause more than its fair share of difficulty. In this event the indicators are not sharp and can lead to poor market timing. This alone is sufficient reason for not buying or holding options during such periods.

For trading near-term options as specified in the above guidelines, the market periods of interest will generally range from four to six weeks in duration. Moreover, under ideal circumstances these periods will occur in long-term bull markets and will coincide with strong intermediate-term uptrends.

Short-term movements in the market usually last from a few days to several weeks. An awareness of these mini-cycles also has its place in market timing, but I've found them most useful for determining initial entry points. It obviously doesn't hurt to register right after checkout time to get first crack at room service!

Short-term indicators often signal changes in market direction so frequently that they're of limited use to the small investor. Playing the tiny ripples on a market indicator is strictly for the big kids.

I'll conclude this portion of the discussion on market environment with perhaps the most important message the Little Guy investor can take away from reading this book. Have patience! Have the patience to wait until you can join in the market action with the best of odds working for you. This cannot be the case without giving adequate consideration to the market environment for the timing of purchases. From personal experience, I know great anxiety can build during the long waiting periods that separate the relatively short periods of favorable market action. This is especially true after coming off successful trades when unlimited confidence is difficult to contain. But straggling back into the market when one should really be on the sidelines can only lead to the attrition of earlier gains. This is hardly a direct route to financial security, although it may eventually lead to early retirement—at least from the market.

Although there are fairly reliable indicators for signaling dramatic changes in market direction, there are also seasonal influences that can and should be used to predict market moves. As one would expect, indicators will confirm whether or not these seasonal factors are actually going to produce a worthwhile upside rally. But for the category of stocks that our guidelines specify, price movements generally tend to lead the way for the rest of the market. As a result, a major move can be well under way in these issues before broad market indicators confirm the overall price action. In particular, we will be concerned with underlying issues that are typically institutional favorites and, as such, tend to be more actively traded at particular times of the year. For example, the ends of March, June, September, and December are quarterly report periods for most institutional funds, and many a portfolio adjustment is made both prior to and after these quarterly deadlines. It's also noteworthy that a majority of quarterly earnings reports are published within a few weeks following these dates. Under proper market conditions the anticipation of favorable earnings can account for additional upside action—although Little Guy beware when the news is announced. Another factor that can generate abnormal price action immediately following the end of the yearly quarters relates to the expiration dates of options themselves. Short sellers who have hedged their positions with options may tend to cover, and the naked option writer may also be called to deliver the underlying stock.

The sum total of these and no doubt many other reasons tends to produce unusual market activity at these four times of the year. Hence, it behooves the aggressive options trader seeking a maximum of leverage to anticipate the potential for gain during these periods. The so-called Santa Claus, or year-end rally, is perhaps the most well-known and consistently predictable stock market rally of all, and it definitely is not a Wall Street myth. In any market environment even remotely bullish at this time of the year, I would recommend taking market action in accordance with the guidelines outlined here. It's the closest one can come to knowing a priori that the odds of winning will be in your favor.

The price of an option almost always moves in the same direction as the price of the underlying stock. In fact, for near-term options that are far into the money, the option and stock prices often move in identical increments with very little premium. Therefore, it's clear that the successful option trader, like his counterpart in the stock market, must be capable of selecting appropriate underlying issues. For the option strategy under consideration here, this skill is put to the test immediately and must prove itself in a relatively short period of time. The trader does not have the luxury (?) of time to bail out bad decisions. Option losses should be taken quickly and by design, but if not, the automatic expiration feature takes charge. There is no such thing as years of prolonged losses in any option position. This is an important point that deserves special emphasis because it relates to a major Little Guy weakness, his inability to time investment sales properly. The rather short life span remaining in near-term options is a great aid for improving performance, since it does not allow for any permanent relationship or sentimental bond to develop between buyer and option. One is strongly compelled to evaluate continuously the extent of an option's prospects during a very brief preexpiration period. The focus of attention centers on the optimum time for sale whether it be to minimize loss or maximize gain. The ever approaching expiration date is also a constant and vivid reminder that all options are terminal cases at best, and one must be prepared for a hasty goodbye on the shortest of notice. Fortunately, most investors seem capable of accepting this urgency for timely action much more readily with option trading than with the disposal of their stock holdings.

Before applying the guidelines for the selection of options, the set of optionable stocks should be screened first to identify the most promising issues. This process is not well defined and is open to subjective analysis followed by large doses of personal interpretation. But if the process were all science and no art, we would all be riding polo ponies to and from the classrooms of Pickawinner Tech.

It's an understatement to say that the general guidelines for selecting optionable stocks can use further elaboration. A convenient starting point for the stock selection process is an evaluation of industry groups. Each industry, be it airlines, computers, drugs, or whatever, rises and falls in public favor much like women's fashions, albeit with greater frequency. These fluctuations in public support are related to business conditions which may or may not be obvious. But fortunately for our short-term purposes, it's only necessary to know which industries are currently up and which are down in popularity.

When a stock is in a popular industry there's a group momentum that rubs off on the individual issues. Although some of these stocks may be getting a free ride, in general the underlying reason for this phenomenon is quite simple. Namely, the broad external forces that influence the business environment, such as government regulations, interest rate changes, etc., are global in effect. They generally tend to favor certain industries and depress others. So the odds dictate that one should pick players only from winning teams.

Ranking industry groups according to their current strength of public support is definitely a job for the computer. No Little Guy could hope to accomplish this on his own in a meaningful way. This information can be obtained from a number of sources; I personally obtain such data from the *Trade Levels Report* mentioned earlier.

The ultimate objective of the stock-screening process is to sort out only those issues that have the potential for making a dramatic upsurge in price within a period of a few weeks. Usually this can only be accomplished with actively traded stocks. High volume is the key to price momentum, and any stock that is not trading well above its average turnover rate is generally not a good candidate for further consideration. As a rule of thumb, one might look for at least a 50 percent increase in the average daily trading volume over the previous month's activity. All too often the lack of increased volume characterizes a drifting price pattern at best.

In selecting active, volatile stocks it should be most encouraging to find such an issue making the current most-active list. Under this condition, upward price momentum may be accelerated even further if the stock has a relatively large outstanding short interest to be worked off during the move. In general, the short interest is considered favorable if it's at least a few percent of the total number of shares outstanding or several times the recent average daily trading volume. Monthly short interest figures are published in the *Wall Street Journal* approximately one week after the fifteenth of each month for a number of actively traded stocks. For other issues, this information can be obtained through your regular broker.

High-flyer glamour stocks, by definition, are the most volatile issues and hence have the greatest potential for making sudden dramatic moves. As mentioned above, these moves are typically, but not always, made on significantly increasing volume. These stocks are generally high-priced institutional favorites that usually trade in large blocks. Without the support of professional money managers, it would be difficult indeed for a stock to attain the price momentum associated with large volume because institutional trading is estimated to account for up to 80 percent of all market transactions. Furthermore, by confining your interest to these active volatile issues, the number of optionable stocks that pass the initial screening will be reduced to a few dozen.

Those underlying stocks that remain for further scrutiny should be examined next for their technical condition. An analysis of company fundamentals is not overly significant here, because the time period of future interest is only a few weeks. Of course, any stock with obvious and disturbingly bad fundamentals should be immediately discarded. But any hidden surprise will probably be revealed in the technical analysis.

It's at this point that the ability to correctly assess daily stock price and volume patterns is most helpful. The simplest approach is to apply basic technical analysis as taught in the most elementary books on reading stock charts.

Recognizing favorable chart patterns, like reading tea leaves, is an art that improves with training and practice. But it's equally important to detect failure patterns, such as the familiar head-and-shoulders configuration, and to steer clear of those stocks that are tracing such formations. Primarily, however, the current chart pattern should never preclude the strong possibility of an immediate upside move with a steep angle of ascent. Ideally, the chart pattern will already be in the early stages of such a move and then continue to follow the same course. But since this is not a book on technical analysis, there is no point to my rambling on. The reader must prepare himself to perform this task.

Other less-direct methods are available for assessing the technical condition of a stock while simultaneously providing timing data for trading. One such method is presented in the next chapter. It is based on combining both price and volume information to determine when the forces of accumulation are about to add upward momentum to a stock's price. The numerical procedures are straightforward but rather time-consuming if applied to a large number of issues. I personally follow eight volatile stocks on a daily basis. This allows me to be prepared in advance when the trading periods arrive, since at least a few of these issues usually satisfy the other criteria for selection. It should be noted, however, that such charting is responsible for nearly all of my formal market preparation time.

Before we leave the subject of stock selection, one qualifying observation should be made regarding industry groups. For those investors who follow and chart a number of volatile stocks, the industry-group rating should not by itself rule out an otherwise acceptable stock, especially if all other factors are highly favorable. The reason for this is that, during the volatile periods of market action that we're trying to anticipate, the ratings of many glamour industries are capable of changing very quickly. During the early stages of any dramatic upsurge in the overall market these volatile, but perhaps latent, groups seem to rally their forces and move from out of nowhere in the ratings to their usual lofty positions.

Next let's turn to the two guidelines for selecting options. Actually they are interrelated for achieving at least two important objectives. For the purpose of this discussion, near-term options will be defined as those about to expire in approximately four to six weeks. For an additional frame of reference, far-out-of-the-money options will have an 8 to

15 percent spread between their exercise and current stock prices. When these two characteristics are combined, the resulting option will generally carry a relatively small premium. In most cases only the volatile nature of the underlying issue keeps the option price above fifty cents, and hence not subject to trading restrictions.

The low price of such options has two important advantages. First of all, the Little Guy with even a few thousand dollars to invest can purchase a fairly large number of options and thereby have an interest in perhaps several hundred thousand dollars worth of stock. For example, it would not be uncommon under our guidelines to put up $2,500 for the purchase of twenty options on an underlying stock selling for $150 per share. Thus, for $2,500 one would at least temporarily control $300,000 worth of stock. Now this is leverage at its finest. It's true the stock must begin to move, and move rather quickly, but if it does you have yourself a first-class winner. It's the daily double, the hard eight, and a wheel all rolled into one great bingo. If you can hit even one of these winners every now and then, you can retire the dinner pail to the attic and replace it with a beach ball.

If this all sounds like a fancy form of gambling, just recall the number of times that you've had a few thousand dollars tied up for years in a go-nowhere stock. In most of these cases there is no way the stocks could have moved up far enough or fast enough to have any significant impact on your lifestyle. But this particular option strategy can, and that's at least part of what investing is all about.

Occasionally option premiums become unusually small even when the options themselves are not far out of the money. For active and volatile stocks this condition is most likely to occur during, or just after, a stock market period characterized by drifting price movement and low volume. Clearly in many of these situations the far-out-of-the-money options guideline can be ignored since its only real purpose is to help assure a low premium. When the latter already exists it may be bonus time.

Another apparent conflict should be noted. Under the above definition of near term, only the January series of options qualifies for purchase in anticipation of market moves at the end of calendar quarters. February and March series, with their later expiration dates, are out of phase and hence may provide less than maximum leverage. But if all other guidelines are satisfied, this near-term requirement can certainly be relaxed somewhat to accommodate otherwise attractive issues. In such cases automatic expiration occurs later than for the January series of options. Unfortunately, this additional time may tempt one to overstay his welcome before being forced to close out positions.

A second advantage also accrues to the options buyer when premiums are low, although for maximum effect it requires some subjective judgment and discipline. Clearly a small ante puts a reasonable limit on the maximum loss that can occur, and this is an important factor. But I certainly wouldn't recommend getting into the action on a go for broke basis. In fact, the astute trader can usually recover most of his ante after the first few weeks if proper price action doesn't develop quickly. It all relates to that corny old saying, I've been so low that everything looks up. In other words, these already low-priced options are slow to deteriorate right up until the last few weeks before expiration, even if they remain 8 to 10 percent out of the money. This is a bonus feature that goes with high-flyer, volatile stocks and should be used to advantage.

A very important word of caution should be given, however, in this regard. When dealing with far-out-of-the-money options involving volatile underlying stocks, it's only a hope factor that props up the option price. The premium can dissipate with a vengeance in the final week prior to expiration unless the option has moved into the money or the stock is rising rapidly toward the exercise price. In these latter cases the option may already show a substantial profit and the trader must be alert to protect his gain. If, at this point, the stock movement seems to stall in the vicinity of the exercise price, my recommendation would be to sell without hesitation, at the current bid price. Take your profit and don't look back on what might have been. All too often it can be depressing.

The general manner in which option prices deteriorate prior to expiration is illustrated in figure 1. In this figure a typical pattern of price decay is demonstrated by plotting contour curves of fixed premium for a hypothetical underlying stock and where the option has an exercise price of $100. The vertical scale measures the number of points, or equivalently, a percentage value that the option is in or out of the money. For example, consider the curve in figure 1 with premium equal to $1. Thirty days from expiration this hypothetical stock is roughly 14 points out of the money. Moving along the curve to the right it can be seen that the stock price must reach the exercise price of $100 approximately one day before expiration. It is at this crossover point through zero on the vertical scale that the option moves into the money. The steep ascent and bunching of curves near the expiration date show graphically how quickly an option price can decrease in the final week even if the stock price remains the same. It's during this period that the option market most resembles the commodity market from the standpoint of high risk. When the stock price drops a point or two in a single day, it's not uncommon for an out-of-the-money option to lose half or more of its value. On the other hand, the contour curves are relatively flat and separated when there are from twenty to thirty trading days remaining before expiration. The implication is that during this period already low premiums are not greatly influenced by the passing of time.

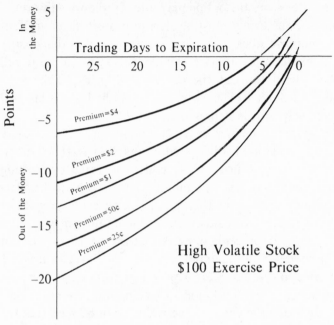

Figure 1. Illustration of Fixed Premium Curve

One of the charting techniques described in the next chapter will provide some assistance on whether or not to sell before the final day of trading. If you have a productive option working for you, it's of utmost importance to stay with it just as long as possible and let your profits continue to multiply. It's similar to finding that super crap shooter who never loses the dice while his winnings are allowed to ride with each successive bet. A few good rolls with one of these shooters can make up for a lot of boxcars and snake eyes after he's gone. Likewise, the option trader must maximize his opportunities.

During these exciting times, especially after an option has moved into the money, the Little Guy's emotions can be stretched to the limit. When net assets can often change by thousands of dollars per day, one must be prepared to deal with the traditional pangs of hope and greed. As long as an option and its underlying stock are rising, hope should always prevail.

Diversification can be an important ingredient of any market strategy, but not always. I can think of at least two exceptions to this rule, and one is usually stated in terms of eggs and baskets. As Gerald Loeb, a famous Wall Street statesman, once said, "Put all your eggs in one basket and then watch the hell out of the basket!" There's a significant message here. With too much diversification you can be lulled into playing down the basic importance of each and every individual position you hold. There's a tendency to get sloppy in your thinking by reasoning that any loss for which there's a corresponding gain is an acceptable one. This rationale may be temporarily comforting, but it's difficult to find a better sample of Little Guy thinking.

There's a second, and to me a more important, factor which relates to diversification. The small investor should never spread his limited resources over so many positions that he can't achieve significant results with the success of just one, and perhaps only one, of his individual selections. Otherwise you're expecting to be right on some sort of average basis, often with no really strong potential on any separate issue. It's even worse if one expects the mediocre results of a number of positions to accumulate into a satisfactory total. So only diversify to the point where your investment stake can support, in both quantity of options and quality of issues, some king-size winners.

Once the decision is made to purchase a given option, it may be prudent to accumulate the total position in two, or at most three, steps. However, if the option is selling for a dollar or less, it's probably best to swallow hard and buy all at once. But otherwise, if there are five or six weeks left before expiration and your overall technical analysis of the short term is inconclusive or somewhat neutral, it may be appropriate to buy, say, one-half of your intended position and then hopefully pyramid up later. This situation arises occasionally when the option price is several dollars per share and the original buy decision is heavily biased by anticipation. It's important in these cases to fill out the total position as quickly as possible, if conditions warrant, so as not to miss any major move with a low entry fee. On the other hand, if the position stalls or deteriorates, one has the alternative of retreating with minimum losses. Generally speaking, I'm inclined to take on the full position in one shot.

Finally, a word or two about taxes. By trading listed options there obviously cannot be any long-term capital gains. But look at it from the positive side. There aren't any long-term capital losses either. In fact, by working only in the short term, tax considerations need never enter into any trading decision except possibly for selling January options. This is the only period when one may be tempted to delay a sale to shift the tax consequence onto the next calendar year. However, even here the successful trader ignores the IRS until it's time to split the loot.

9

Market Indicators and Other Technical Tools

The previous chapter presented guidelines for trading options with maximum leverage. Of necessity, this discussion was less than specific in outlining the thought processes and screening procedures that should be used to arrive at one's investment decisions. Clearly there cannot be a regimented approach for consistently applying these guidelines successfully, especially in the area of selecting optionable stocks. But execution of the guidelines need not be left entirely to personal judgment. All too often this leads to market actions based on false optimism or, put another way, unfounded anticipation. Fortunately, there are market indicators and timing tools that can help eliminate some of the uncertainty. These indicators are based on impersonal, well-defined technical measurements and often provide a valid and objective rationale for market action. Without them, the small investor is left entirely on his own to reconcile his many emotions with subjective analysis.

No market indicator seems to work well all the time, and there are certainly more than enough to choose from with a variety of objectives. So it's important to confine one's attention to a manageable few and only adopt those that prove to be most reliable. In many cases more than one indicator for a given purpose simply provides redundant or, worse yet, conflicting information. In the latter case they frequently confuse the true picture and become all but useless. Redundant indicators seem to be most valuable when there are only two and they tend to confirm each other for market timing. Perhaps the best-known example of this is the classical Dow Theory discussed in most traditional market textbooks. Without this confirmation feature, maintaining redundant indicators is often nothing more than a manifestation of market frustration.

I'm now a dedicated advocate of keeping market analysis and preparation as simple as possible. I make use of only a handful of different indicators and other technical tools. Even among this limited set, I draw upon my weekly *Trade Levels Report* for a number of graphical presentations and underlying numerical calculations. In this way I minimize the amount of personal charting required while staying abreast of the current market environment. Let's face it—charting's a bore!

Market indicators are often classified by the type of entity they attempt to measure. In this chapter, two different types relating to market timing are discussed. The two categories involve the determination of market strength and of investor sentiment. A third timing tool to be described measures the forces of accumulation and distribution which act on the price movement of a particular stock. Generally speaking, by accumulation we mean here the net acquisition of a stock either before or during a substantial price rise, whereas distribution relates to the net sale of an issue before or during a price decline.

Indicators for assessing the general market environment will be discussed first. To determine market condition, either long, intermediate, or short term, some fundamental and relatively sensitive market variable must be chosen as the basis for measuring market strength. Among the possible alternatives, market *breadth* wins the honors. For definition, a daily breadth measurement B is simply the net number of advancing issues A over those declining D on the New York Stock Exchange (NYSE). In a symbolic notation:

$$B_n = A_n - D_n.$$

The subscript n denotes day number n. This value can be either positive or negative depending on the relative sizes of A_n and D_n. From here on the following definitions of three indicators for characterizing the long-, short-, and intermediate-term condition of the market are by courtesy of Trade Levels, Inc. A few of the later descriptive remarks are based on my personal interpretation and I assume full blame for any resulting confusion.

As additional notation let $(STI)_n$, $(ITI)_n$, and $(LTI)_n$ denote the short-, intermediate-, and long-term indicators respectively, calculated for day n. Then on the following day $(n+1)$ the three indicators are given by:

$$(STI)_{n+1} = \frac{(STI)_n + B_n}{2} \quad (50\% \text{ index})$$

$$(ITI)_{n+1} = \frac{9(ITI)_n + B_n}{10} \quad (10\% \text{ index})$$

$$(LTI)_{n+1} = \frac{99(LTI)_n + B_n}{100} \quad (1\% \text{ index}).$$

In the *Trade Levels Report* each of these values is referred to as a Haurlan Index for the short, intermediate, and long term. The naming convention is for the president of Trade Levels, Inc., Peter N. Haurlan. Clearly, these three indices represent daily, moving averages of NYSE breadth. Each index is weighted such that the older the data, the less effect they have.

If one begins to calculate these indicators without accurate initial values, a zero starting value may be used. But in this case, a period of time must elapse before the indicators stabilize. The time periods required are 3, 20, and 200 days for the short, intermediate, and long terms respectively. These three spans reflect the number of accumulated data points that influence each respective index. All three indicators are plotted each week in the *Trade Levels Report* and are accompanied by a descriptive analysis.

These three breadth indicators are useful for assessing the overall market environment. In general the environment is positive when they are positive and negative when they are negative. The signal for a change in market direction is typically given when they pass through zero. However, to avoid whipsaws with short- and intermediate-term buy and sell signals, the indicators are usually required to pass well beyond zero. In particular, short-term buy and sell signals are generated when the index passes upward through +100 and downward through −150 respectively. For the intermediate term, offsets are determined by the local chart pattern.

The long-term condition of the market is best evaluated by applying basic technical analysis to the LTI chart pattern extended back over a period of several years. This indicator tends to change rather slowly and reflects the long-term trend quite well. As pointed out in chapter 7, however, long-term bull or bear markets usually reverse direction only after playing out a well-worn scenario of business stages or cycles. Hence, an awareness of the general business climate, together with a chart of the *LTI* indicator, is usually more than adequate to predict when the final curtain is going to fall on the last animal act, be it bull or bear.

The *STI* gives a buy or sell signal following sufficient changes in market breadth. But occasionally it's useful to anticipate when these signals might occur. For this purpose I've compiled statistics on the NYSE over the past few years that estimate the probability of the current market environment, whether positive or negative, carrying over from one day to the next. For the purpose of characterizing a positive market, the following closing features are used: positive breadth, positive change in the Dow-Jones industrial average, increase in average stock price, and a strong market close. Actually only three out of four of these conditions need apply for defining a positive day. A negative market environment lacks at least three of these features.

The statistical data are summarized in figure 2. The vertical scale represents the probability of at least *n* consecutive days of consistent market action, either positive or negative. For example, the probability that the market will change from positive to negative, or vice versa, after three successive days of similar action is $100 - 28 = 72$ percent. These probabilities reflect the so-called rubber band or snap back principle of short-term market behavior. According to this rather simple but descriptive theory, when the market moves the same way on consecutive days, counteracting market forces build up and eventually cause a snap back to the opposite direction. No doubt this is actually just a fancy way of saying that profit takers and bargain hunters are alternately doing their number on all us Little Guys.

The chart of figure 2 can be used to bolster one's confidence while fine tuning entry and exit points into and out of the market. It's uncomfortably hard on a person's pride

to have a newly acquired option suddenly take a dive
shortly after its purchase, or conversely to soar after a sale.
Yet, for example, it usually takes a number of up days for
the small investor to muster the courage to place a buy
order. By this time profit takers are already circling
overhead waiting their turn to snatch the telltale confirmation slip as it hits your broker's in-basket.

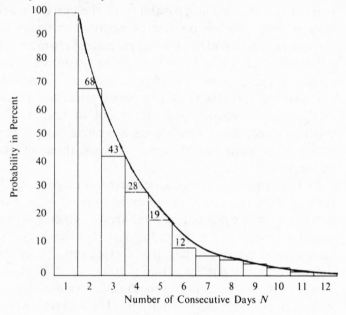

Figure 2. Probability of at Least N Consecutive
Days of Similar Market Action

Another technical tool I follow with interest is called the
McClellan Oscillator. It was developed by Sherman and
Marion McClellan of Los Angeles, California, and it too is
included in the *Trade Levels Report*. This leading indicator varies up and down through zero and generally
remains between limits of ±200 points. A chart of this
indicator for a period of several years is in figure 3. When
this oscillator is above +100 or below −100, the market

is usually considered to be overbought or oversold respectively.

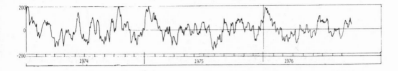

Figure 3. The McClellan Oscillator
(Courtesy Trade Levels, Inc.)

To define the McClellan Oscillator (MO), another value, called the 5 percent index, is required:

$$(FPI)_{n+1} = \frac{95(FPI)_n + 5N_n}{100} \quad (5\% \text{ index}).$$

Then for day n, the oscillator is given by:

$$MO_n = ITI_n - FPI_n.$$

I prefer to relate this value of MO_n with the velocity of market strength. When MO is large and positive the overall market is rising sharply; when it's large negatively, stand by for a crash dive. Actually, the identification of the McClellan Oscillator with a velocity component can be justified on the basis of its construction as the difference between two estimates of market strength. But even with the lack of a rigorous mathematical derivation it's conceptionally advantageous to think in terms of velocity when considering the next and more important indicator, the Summation Index.

The Summation Index (SI) is a market indicator computed daily by adding the current value of the McClellan Oscillator with the sum of all previous values. The initial starting date for the summation is somewhat immaterial in that it only affects a vertical offset in the resulting chart pattern. Symbolically,

$$SI_n = SI_{n-1} + MO_n$$

$$= \sum_{k}^{n} MO_k .$$

In mathematical terms this can then be considered the integration of a velocity component (the rate of change of market strength) to obtain market strength. A chart of this Summation Index gives a much better insight into market condition since it displays strength directly. A graph of this index from mid-1975 to late 1976 appears in figure 4. The chart data have been made available by Mr. and Mrs. McClellan, and with the assistance of Gene Morgan, who summarizes a broad set of market statistics daily on Los Angeles financial television Channel 22.

The Summation Index can be used with great effectiveness for detecting turns in market direction. At least this has been my personal, although somewhat limited, experience. I describe it in the next chapter. The chart pattern in figure 4 has well-defined local tops and bottoms separated by periods of rising and falling market strength. Basically, this index is an intermediate-term indicator. The lack of frequent oscillations in the data makes buy and sell signals, based on the reversals of market strength, much more reliable. Hence undesirable whipsaw action is minimal.

The indicators discussed up to this point are all derived from underlying measurements of market breadth. A different type of index based on a measure of investor sentiment is presented next.

Throughout my experience of following the market in close detail, I have always maintained a special interest in the way the market closes. I discovered early on that, when it closed weak, I generally found myself with a pessimistic attitude; on a strong close I was ready to buy everything in

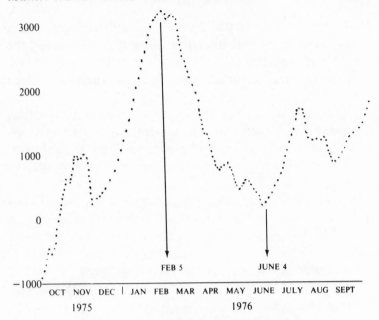

Figure 4. The Summation Index
(Courtesy of Sherman and Marian McClellan)

sight. It finally occurred to me that this cause-and-effect relationship might apply equally well in reverse. That is, the overriding factor that actually made for a strong or weak close was precisely investor sentiment toward the current market. Using this premise, I selected a market statistic that I felt best described the NYSE close, regardless of whether it was vigorous, lackluster, or downright disheartening. For this purpose I chose the final closing *Tick* figure.

The Tick is a market statistic that changes throughout the course of a daily trading session and is defined as follows: At a given point in time, the number of stocks that have decreased in price on their last trade of the day is subtracted from the number of issues that have increased in price on their last trade. This net value, either positive or negative, is the current Tick. It's one of the few market statistics not related to the previous day's activity. For the purpose of developing figure 2, a positive closing Tick is equivalent to my definition of a strong close. However, the magnitude of the closing Tick is clearly important for assessing relative market strength or weakness on a given day.

I usually obtain the closing Tick figure from the final summary of market statistics presented on financial television. This value may also be obtained from a number of financial reporting systems that tie into local brokerage houses.

In developing this sentiment indicator, the closing Tick is first converted into the form of an oscillator. As in forming the McClellan Oscillator, this accomplishes two purposes: First, the raw Tick data are subject to a smoothing process, and secondly, one obtains a velocity component for market sentiment. The latter, of course, can be equated with market strength.

The Tick Oscillator (TO) is derived in a manner similar to that for the McClellan Oscillator. If T_n is the closing Tick value on day n, then—

$$A_n = \frac{9A_{n-1} + T_n}{10} \quad (10\% \text{ index})$$

$$C_n = \frac{95B_{n-1} + 5T_n}{100} \quad (5\% \text{ index})$$

and $TO_n = A_n - C_n.$ (Tick Oscillator)

If initial values for A_n and C_n are not available, they may be assumed zero. As with the Haurlan Indices, these values eventually converge to proper values with the passing of sufficient time.

The Tick Oscillator may be interpreted in much the same way as the McClellan Oscillator, namely, as a velocity component of market strength. It generally moves up and down through zero, and except for very strong or very weak markets, it usually remains in the range of ±60 points. A notable exception to these limits is illustrated in figure 5 where the Tick Oscillator approached +100 during the strong market upsurge that took place during the Santa Claus rally of 1975–76.

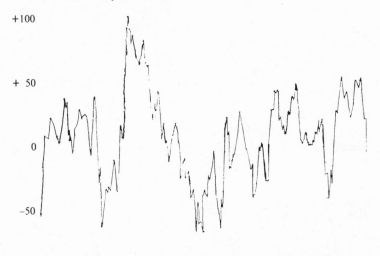

Figure 5. Tick Oscillator

When the current value of the Tick Oscillator is added to the sum of all previous values, one obtains the Tick Summation Index (TSI). Symbolically,

$$TSI_n = TSI_{n-1} + TO_n$$

$$= \sum_k^n TO_k.$$

As with the regular Summation Index this indicator also gives a direct measure of market strength. A chart of TSI appears in figure 6 for the same time period covered in figure 4. The similarity of the two chart patterns is evident. It's interesting to note that the market top occurring in February 1976 was realized on February 5 using the regular Summation Index and on February 25 with the Tick Summation. My own personal market results during this period are discussed in the next chapter. For my portfolio of options, the February 25 date was ideal for confirming the earlier sell signal given on February 5.

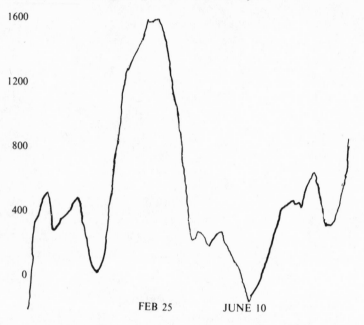

Figure 6. Tick Summation Index

It may be well, at this point, to pause and summarize how I use the indicators described thus far. The three Haurlan indices are used primarily for assessing the overall market environment and, with the possible exception of the short-term index, they are never used to provide buy and sell signals. This doesn't mean I'm trying to minimize their value, since it is important to be aware of the long-term trend and be an active buyer only when intermediate-term market conditions are favorable. The short-term condition, however, can be a somewhat different matter. As pointed out in the previous chapter, there are times when one may want to anticipate those short-term, dynamic market moves that often occur near the end of yearly quarters. At these times, an option purchase made in accordance with the trading guidelines, but without a formal buy flash from the Haurlan short-term index, generally poses little risk during the first week or two that it's held. This allows one to get on board early for the entire ride should the market suddenly perk up. If not, the Haurlan Index won't confirm the buy decision and the position can always be closed.

Anticipation is not always a good substitute for a technical indicator that flashes go. So there will be times when one may prefer a formal invitation to join the action. When a sell signal is generated by the Haurlan short-term index, and options populate your portfolio, it's definitely a time for caution, but not panic. Since short-term swings can make a round trip in a matter of just a few days, it's important not to automatically surrender any position with remaining upside potential. Very shortly in this chapter there will be a discussion on how one can arrive at these troublesome sell decisions without undue trauma.

The only buy signal that I currently look for, and will tend to act upon, is that generated when the Tick Summation Index and the regular Summation Index confirm one another in a reversal of market strength to the upside. As long as both of these indicators continue to move upward I consider the market environment to be favorable for buying and/or holding options. During these periods I still try to coordinate my purchases with the guideline for selecting near-term options. However, if this buy signal remains in effect after the near-term options have expired, I don't rule out the possibility of rolling over my positions to the next expiration month or turn to other near-term issues.

When the Summation Index and the Tick Summation Index both confirm a reversal of market strength to the downside, it's time to start gathering up the well-worn hat and coat. This is definitely an intermediate-term sell signal, and from here on in it should only be a matter of proceeding in an orderly fashion to the exit.

The final technical tool that I use in my market preparation attempts to illustrate and predict how forces of accumulation and distribution will influence the movement of stock prices. The basic charting procedures were developed by Larry Williams and first came to my attention in 1973 as an article in *The 1973 Stock Traders Almanac,* (see chapter 10). In the discussion below, his terminology is retained.

Accumulation and distribution for an individual stock is approximated by the expression:

$$S = \frac{\triangle}{H-L} *V$$

where $\triangle$ is the net daily price change, V is the daily volume traded and H-L is the difference between the daily high and low prices. (Actually Williams' formula uses the difference between the stock's closing and opening prices instead of $\triangle$.) The value of this expression denotes net accumulation or distribution depending on whether it is positive or negative. For computational convenience I always round off this volume quantity to the nearest 500 shares.

The value of S is summed on a daily basis to obtain a cumulative total. The resulting data are then smoothed by calculating a three-day moving average denoted by C. When plotted on an appropriate scale, these values of C provide a *Cumulative Line.*

Next, a ten-day moving average of points on the Cumulative Line is used to further smooth the data and obtain a longer-term trend T. The difference $P=C$-T defines a *Pressure* curve and the ten-day moving average of P is called the *Momentum* line M. Both P and M are plotted on the same scale, a different scale from C. Generally P and M vary between limits of $\pm 3{,}000$.

If the charting procedures described above in rapid succession seem overly confusing on the first pass, don't be too concerned. The notation unscrambles quite readily if and when you attempt to do some actual charting. As an example, figure 7 contains curves *C, P,* and *M* for Digital Equipment Corporation during a two-month span in mid-1976.

For an interpretation of these three curves, the Cumulative Line *C* is a direct representation of net accumulation or distribution. A necessary, but not sufficient, condition for a buy signal to be generated is that this line be increasing. Ideally, it will be starting to increase after a decline. The Pressure and Momentum curves reflect short- and somewhat-longer-term forces respectively. The *P* curve cuts through the *M* curve in a wavelike pattern, causing a subsequent and similar motion in *M,* although of much smaller amplitude and frequency. Conceptually, one can consider *P* as a force (pressure) that bends *M* in the direction that *P* is moving.

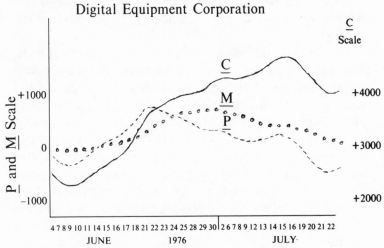

Digital Equipment Corporation

Figure 7. Accumulation/Distribution Chart for DEC

Momentum forces due to accumulation or distribution are of primary importance for assessing the advisability of purchasing or holding an option on the underlying stock. Pressure forces are important too, but more for kicking off the price movement. Hence, in addition to a favorable Cumulative Line, a buy signal is generated for me when the Pressure curve P is increasing and about to intersect M on the upside. As long as P remains above M the resulting option purchase is generally a hold. Sell signals are theoretically generated when the above conditions and relationships between curves P and M are reversed.

The charting procedures outlined above are an associate tool to be used with, not as a substitute for, the technical analysis mentioned in the preceding chapter. In particular, it should be stressed that the Cumulative Line reflects net accumulation and distribution, not price action. Hence, I don't always act immediately on the sell signals that are generated. But if a stock and its associated option begin to drop in price after such a signal, it's usually time to sell. In any questionable cases, especially when the option is still out of the money and expiration is close at hand, one can check the relative position of P and M. If P is below M and not moving upward, my judgment is to sell and to act pronto.

This ends the discussion of indicators and technical tools. They're the only ones I use, and they are not time consuming to maintain. Although I would be less than candid if I gave the impression that they're foolproof, I've never found or developed a better set. I believe it's accurate to say that the real beauty of these tools lies in their relative simplicity and well-defined signals. In an investment world overflowing with limp handshakes and soft market counsel, they provide a few solid handles to grasp while pulling out of the mire of uncertainty. Some personal experience with the use of these technical tools is presented in the following chapter.

10

Reviewing the Evidence

By December 1975, I had settled on a number of basic features for an option-trading strategy and was more than anxious to put them to the test. In no way, however, was I prepared with a unified trading approach with all the ingredients and precautions outlined in the previous two chapters. In my eagerness to join in the action, my thinking was biased almost entirely toward the purchase of options. Initially, at least, there was very little thought given to the possibility of retreating from any positions, much less to such mundane matters as establishing selling thresholds or planning for a hasty withdrawal. Actually, the overall situation was further complicated by my Little Guy thinking which was still under house arrest. It remained with me after all my brainwashing attempts to help it escape.

The more experience I gained in the option market, however, the better I was able to evaluate my performance and refine the trading procedures. The net operating results accumulated to date are reflected in my current trading philosophy as already outlined.

In retrospect, the development period was highly gratifying, and yet at times it was characterized by unnecessary frustration. The latter occurred whenever I allowed myself to disregard the market environment that was unfolding. It's one thing to gloss over pessimistic market commentary and downside action on the Dow; it's another to accept increasing portfolio losses. But a more important shortcoming was revealed on those occasions when I ignored the most obvious action signals provided by my indicators. It was like cramming for an exam and then missing the test. At other times I neglected a related trading principle: When sell signals are generated, they're only useful in the option market if defensive action is taken rather quickly. Almost any delay can be costly as I respectfully learned.

My first option-trading period was set solely in anticipation of a year-end rally in late 1975. The market had been moving in a rather narrow trading range for several months, and, without consulting any indicators for a buy signal, I simply stepped up and placed my bets. This initial entry into the option market, even using my preliminary trading guidelines, produced exceptional financial results and served to reinforce my earlier convictions on the value of this new approach.

My option portfolio during this test period of approximately five weeks is presented in table 2. In addition to demonstrating some of the major points discussed in earlier chapters, it also illustrates the type of records I maintain on a daily basis. Under each option listed in table 2, three items are recorded each day: closing price, trading volume

DEC/JAN
1975/1976

DATE	DECAD	DECAH	TGRBB	TSODC	XRXDL	Totals Daily	Acc.
12/10	$\oplus 10^{1/220}_{-25}$					-25	
12/11	$7^{1/366}_{-250}$					-250	-275
12/12	$7^{1/241}\,25$					25	-250
12/15	$8^{1/118}\,50$					50	-200
12/16	$\oplus 11^{/442}325$					325	150
12/17	$12^{/224}200$	$\bullet 1\frac{1}{16}\,245_{-40}$				160	310
12/18	$12^{1/285}150$	$\star 1\frac{11}{16}\,262\,350$				500	810
12/19	$11^{/265}_{-350}$	$1^{1/239}_{-845}$				-1195	-385
12/22	$9^{1/159}_{-300}$	$0^{1/137}_{-565}$				-965	-1350
12/23	$12^{1/341}650$	$1^{1/216}750$				1400	50
12/24	$15^{/210}450$	$\star 1^{1/322}630$				1080	1130
12/26	$19^{/207}800$	$3^{/254}2500$				3300	4430
12/29	$17^{1/340}_{-300}$	$\bullet 2^{1/538}_{-1475}$	$\square 0^{1/357}_{-220}$			-1995	2435
12/30	$16^{1/178}_{-125}$	$2^{1/364}_{-1500}$	$0\frac{1}{16}\,91_{-250}$			-1875	560
12/31	$17^{1/245}50$	$2^{1/460}375$	$0^{1/103}250$			675	1235
1/2	$+17^{/165}_{-100}$	$2^{1/389}1125$	$\bullet 0^{1/272}1500$			2525	3760
1/5		$\bullet 3^{/742}1010$	$0^{1/132}_{-625}$	$\boxtimes 1\frac{5}{16}\,902_{-25}$		360	4120
1/6		$3^{1/1185}2000$	$0\frac{13}{16}\,330310$	$1\frac{1}{16}\,617_{-400}$		1910	6030
1/7		$3^{1/1496}1500$	$0^{1/778}_{-310}$	$1\frac{1}{16}\,3890$		1190	7220
1/8		$\dagger 4^{1/1254}1750$	$0^{1/227}0$	$1\frac{1}{16}\,3340$		1750	8970
1/9		$7^{1/1490}5250$	$0^{1/124}_{-625}$	$1\frac{1}{16}\,3150$	$\bullet 2\frac{5}{16}\,1219_{-110}$	4515	13485
1/12		$10^{1/920}6000$	$0^{1/237}625$	$1\frac{1}{16}\,392200$	$\diamond 2^{1/1473}1000$	7825	21310
1/13		$10^{1/749}1500$	$0^{1/358}_{-625}$	$1\frac{1}{16}\,373_{-200}$	n/a	675	21985
1/14		$\blacksquare 18^{/533}13000$	$0\frac{13}{16}\,373935$	$1^{1/379}200$	$3^{1/1291}1125$	15260	37245
1/15		$\blacksquare 16^{1/411}_{-1510}$	$0^{1/521}_{-315}$	$1^{1/505}0$	$2\frac{5}{16}\,1422_{-1685}$	-3510	33735
1/16			$0\frac{13}{16}\,179315$	$1^{1/386}0$	$2\frac{5}{16}\,8500$	315	34050

⊕ BUY 1 OPTION   ◇ BUY 20 OPTIONS
★ BUY 5 OPTIONS   + SELL 2 OPTIONS
• BUY 10 OPTIONS   ■ SELL 10 OPTIONS
□ BUY 40 OPTIONS   † SELL 20 OPTIONS
⊠ BUY 16 OPTIONS

Table 2. Option Trading Results for December/January, 1975–76

in number of options, and the dollar change resulting from daily price movement. In the two right-hand columns I place the net daily price change over all positions, together with the accumulated sum of these changes. Dollar values recorded always include commission costs incurred by adding or deleting positions and hence the accumulated sum represents a true net capital gain figure. Such portfolio changes are then flagged with a footnote so I can readily reconstruct all transactions. As a final record-keeping procedure, I always record negative results in red and positive ones in black. This allows me to assess my trading performance in living color with only a fleeting glance. Now I know why bulls hate the sight of red!

It can be seen from table 2 that I entered the options market slowly and with little diversification. Digital Equipment Corporation satisfied my criteria for optionable stocks, and I entered into small positions with both the January 120 (DECAD) and January 140 (DECAH) options. As these issues increased in value I doubled my position in DECAD to two and eventually raised my holding in DECAH to forty. Toward the end of December, I also added forty Tiger International February 10 options (TGRBB).

By the end of the year my portfolio not only showed a small accumulated gain, but I was well positioned to take advantage of any final upside action in DEC before the January 16 expiration date. On January 2 I sold my two DECAD options for a 70 percent gain, and shifted the proceeds into additional DECAH's since this is where the greatest leverage remained. Other options purchased during this trading period were sixteen Tesoro Petroleum April 15s (TSODC) and thirty Xerox April 60s (XRXDL). With such little time remaining in the January options, and with a strong market environment, I relaxed my near-term guideline and shifted to April options for these latter purchases.

But enough of this dialogue on how and what positions I assembled. It's more important and instructive to relate the manner in which I disposed of the forty DECAH options. To begin with, in early January, Digital Equipment stock made an 18-point move within a two-week period. While the stock traveled from 138 to 156, the DECAH option surged from 2⅝ to as high as 18. If this all sounds familiar, it is! As mentioned in chapter 6, a similar dynamic move was made by both DEC and the October 120 option during the previous October. But once again my Little Guy emotions prevailed and I finally settled for half a loaf.

It can be seen from the accumulated total in table 2 that, starting in January, the value of my portfolio was increasing rapidly and that most of this increase was due to DECAH. It was easy to accept these positive daily changes to my assets until I started to contemplate how quickly my good fortune could reverse with a setback in DEC. After all, this one position represented a large percentage value of my portfolio. Finally, on January 8, when the stock had an early morning pullback, I panicked and nervously sold off half of my position at 3⅞. However, by the end of trading, the option closed at 4⅞ and my Little Guy thinking had deprived me of an additional $2,000 daily gain. This was bad enough, but it hurts even more when I recall that the ride in DEC had only begun.

In fairness to my more mature instincts, I disposed of the remaining DECAH options in an orderly and rather optimal fashion. All the other options in my portfolio remained dormant for the most part during this period, but before the month of January was over even they came to life. The net gain for the trading period covered in table 2 represented over a 260 percent return on my maximum investment.

The overall results obtained during this trading period were gratifying to say the least. Clearly, an important lesson to be learned from it all was never to sell a position without a good technical reason. But this dictate only points up the need for an appropriate selling strategy. No strategy is usually the worst strategy, and it can be a disastrous void in any game plan not to have one. Looking back, one can only conclude that I was fortunate that the strong positive market environment carried me through this trading period since I was ill prepared for defensive action. But on the other hand, it also emphasizes the importance of operating only against the background of a highly favorable market. It's no secret that market strength is the best offset for human weakness.

For the next several months I continued to participate in the option market, adding new positions and generally basking in my newfound success. I also became careless in applying even my preliminary guidelines, and by the end of the first quarter I was holding eight different positions in anticipation of a new market surge that never materialized. Worse yet, I had surrendered nearly 20 percent of my earlier gains by relying on raw hope instead of sound trading principles. At this point, I still hadn't constructed a meaningful selling strategy based on technical tools, much less on common sense. In particular, had I made use of the Summation Indices of chapter 9 for action signals, I would have eliminated all my positions on February 26 and remained a spectator until after June 11. On these dates the two indicators gave confirmation of a change in market direction. Without belaboring the details, I can testify on the basis of this experience that the options market is definitely no place for hanging around between major up moves. Furthermore, had I followed the February 26 sell

DATE	DECGN			DECGP			RCAGF			Totals Daily	Acc.
6/16	⋆3/	267	205							205	
6/17	⋆4¹/	502	485	‡1¹⁄₁₆	293	-230				255	460
6/18	4⁵/	591	1000	■1⁷⁄₁₆	444	-270				730	1190
6/21	8/	1104	5200	‡2¹/	792	3725				8925	10115
6/22	6⁵/	935	-2400	⊠2³/	1320	-1585				-3985	6130
6/23	8⁵/	724	3400	4/	889	5200				8600	14730
6/24	9¹/	845	2000	3¹/	1052	-400	◊0⁷⁄₁₆	300	130	1730	16460
6/25	7⁵/	507	-3400	3/	562	-2800	0⁵⁄₁₆	n/a	-500	-6700	9760
6/28	8/	303	400	2¹/	336	-400	0¹/	487	-250	-250	9510
6/29	8⁵/	425	1000	3¹/	426	1200	0⁷⁄₁₆	1026	750	2950	12460
6/30	8⁵/	890	200	3/	856	-800	0⁵⁄₁₆	1316	500	-100	12360
7/1	7⁵/	429	-1600	2¹/	595	-2000	0¹/	401	-750	-4350	8010
7/2	8¹/	301	600	2¹/	293	0	0¹/	429	0	600	8610
7/6	6⁵/	379	-2000	1¹/	482	-2400	0⁵⁄₁₆	304	-250	-4650	3960
7/7	9¹/	495	4200	2¹/	825	3200	0⁵⁄₁₆	365	0	7400	11360
7/8	8⁵/	622	-1400	2/	998	-2000	0⁵⁄₁₆	224	-500	-3900	7460
7/9	10¹/	704	3000	2¹⁵⁄₁₆	982	3000	0¹/	961	250	6250	13710
7/12	12/	374	2400	2¹/	966	-200	0¹/	520	-500	1700	15410
7/13	8⁵/	457	-5200	1¹/	1072	-5200	0¹/	1693	0	-10400	5010
7/14	+8¹/	389	-660	1⁵⁄₁₆	916	-200	⊕0⁵⁄₁₆	2208	115	-745	4265
7/15				⊖0⁵⁄₁₆	846	-2865				-2865	1400
7/16				•0⁵⁄₁₆	662	-130				-130	1270

⋆ BUY 8 DECGN   + SELL 16 DECGN
‡ BUY 8 DECGP   ⊖ SELL 22 DECGP
■ BUY 10 DECGP   • SELL 10 DECGP
◊ BUY 40 RCAGF   ⊕ SELL 40 RCAGF
⊠ BUY 6 DECGP

Table 3. Option Trading Results for June–July, 1976

signal, I would have recorded a net capital gain during this early 1976 period of $68,510. This would be a 530 percent return on my maximum out-of-pocket investment.

By the time a new market upturn was confirmed on June 11, I realized that a successful options strategy must be based more on solid technical analysis than on luck and anticipation. I recognized this confirmation signal for what it was and prepared to take advantage of a potential midyear rally. Within a few days I opened new positions in Digital Equipment (again) and RCA July options as indicated in table 3. The numbers tell the story more vividly than any words. What Wall Street giveth in June, it taketh away in July. And about the only consolation I can take from this trading period is that I was subsequently able to add some substance to my overall approach to selling.

Beginning July 1 my options positions began to deteriorate badly. After resting briefly for a few days they again resumed their downward trend. The final week before expiration was an all-out catastrophe. I managed to salvage a slight gain for the entire period by selling the sixteen DECGN options before they too disintegrated. Fortunately, I was well aware that the July 170 option (DECGN) was moving nearly one-for-one in price with the stock. And with DEC behaving poorly the relatively large dollar value of this holding was in jeopardy. On the other hand, the July 180 option (DECGP) never moved very far into the money and remained rather low priced. Working with these small numbers somehow promoted a false sense of well-being and at a time when I should have been a nervous Nelly. This was a perfect illustration of how quickly out-of-the-money options can lose their value while waiting out the last few days before expiration. During this five-day period DEC itself slid from 181 to 172½, leaving me with stunned disbelief at such a quick reversal.

Meanwhile, the DECGP option never broke stride as it raced headlong for the nearest cellar.

After assembling this unbelievable one-week loss, I forced myself through an unpleasant, but enlightening, postmortem. Analyzing the climactic breakdown in the DECGP option eventually led to the development of figure 1 in chapter 8, and I soon began to understand with vivid clarity the risk side of holding out-of-the-money options. At the same time I searched for a technical tool that could have assisted me in making an early sell decision, rather than simply waiting for a last-minute, miraculous turnaround in price action. One tentative solution was close at hand. For any significant rebound the underlying stock would most likely need strong support from the forces of accumulation even if current prices weren't increasing. But I was already charting this information, at least for DEC, and had completely ignored it. A look back at figure 7 is most revealing when correlated with the results of table 2. From June 25 on, the Pressure Curve remained below Momentum and indicated a weak configuration for the forces of accumulation. Even the Cumulative Line *C* flattened out in early July, peaked on the fourteenth, and then began a rather noticeable decline. Clearly, this evidence, properly observed, could have provided the corroboration necessary to produce a sell decision well in advance of those last few days of destruction.

The preliminary results obtained from this rather brief testing period are certainly far from conclusive. Nevertheless, I firmly believe they substantiate the remarks set forth in chapter 1 regarding the small investor's only real chance for achieving large capital gains. If my own personal experience is any indication, there may, however, be one major flaw in applying this overall approach to options trading. This deficiency could lie in the potentially false assumption that the Little Guy can, in fact, stop acting like one. The ability to control one's emotions and strictly adhere to sound trading principles is essential and can't be overstated. This includes not only following the guidelines for purchasing options, but the preparation of an adequate defensive strategy. Any oversight or mistake made on the purchase end must be quickly detected and then corrected even faster. Otherwise the inherent risks associated with unhedged option purchases can be overwhelming, and they usually are.

It's often said that one of the most difficult market actions for a small investor to take is selling. The reasons behind this observation are numerous and not very flattering. Yet, selling a security rarely receives the attention it deserves, even though it's clearly just as important, if not more so, than establishing new positions. There's no point in having a well-planned and smooth take-off only to settle for a bumpy or crash landing.

For the most part, my own recommendations for closing options positions have already been discussed in earlier chapters. To provide additional emphasis, however, some of the firmer procedures are also summarized below.

1. When the Summation Index and the Tick Summation Index confirm one another on a reversal of market strength, sell all positions as quickly as possible.
2. Sell all out-of-the-money options at least one week before expiration unless the underlying stock price is increasing rapidly and the forces of accumulation are in a positive configuration. When in doubt, sell.
3. Never sell an in-the-money option without a good technical reason.
4. Sell all options by early morning of the last trading day before expiration.

These selling principles must be coordinated, of course, with a close watch on the technical condition of the underlying stocks. Also, one shouldn't hesitate to set mental stops on either options or their stocks to limit downside risk and avoid unacceptable losses. In any event, it's always a step in the right direction to have some defensive strategy, whatever it may be. This is one area where playing by ear can quickly land you on it.

But, if the small investor can muster sufficient self-discipline and suppress his Little Guy emotions, there's new hope in sight for successful investing. Initially, a few eyebrows may be raised, including your own, as the options guidelines are applied with positive results. And don't be concerned about that strange new feeling you experience; it will be that of a winner.

11

Staying Active in the Off Seasons

Every bull market eventually comes to an end, and the long-term trend of stock prices turns downward. Likewise intermediate-term rallies also have a lifespan of their own whether they occur in bull or bear markets. As simple as these statements appear, the successful trader always has them in mind. The importance of recognizing the termination of uptrends has already been emphasized in previous chapters, and the option buyer must remain alert for technical sell signals as they are generated.

Periods of major market strength such as the year-end rally of 1975 rarely occur. Significant up moves of lesser magnitude, although somewhat more frequent, are also relatively short lived. These same comments apply equally well to periods of market weakness. However, much of the time the market either drifts with a slight bias up or down, or else oscillates back and forth in a wavelike motion within a trading range. Neither of these situations is appropriate, much less ideal, for the purchase or retention of call options. In the first case, time is a deadly enemy, especially with out-of-the-money options. In the latter environment, it's often difficult to trade on peaks and valleys without generating, at best, minor gains for the investor and major commission income for the broker. So what should the options buyer do during these lackluster periods? Go fishing! And don't hesitate to renew your license just as often as necessary.

It has long been a personal observation that most small investors are reluctant to assume any kind of negative market posture. This includes both short sales in the stock market and writing naked options. One reason for this may be the perpetual facade of optimism displayed by the brokerage community. Only the risk side of short positions is emphasized, if the subject is mentioned at all. One is constantly reminded that short sale losses are potentially unlimited since stock prices can theoretically rise without bound. For greater shock value the phrase *go to infinity* is often used. It may be a great catch phrase, but it is hardly realistic. How many times have you ever heard of a stock going out of sight? Put me down for never. There is also a demeaning undertone to the assumption that the Little Guy would be frozen into inaction while his liabilities approached disastrous levels. On the contrary, although the small investor may be the worst offender in letting losses grow on the downside, his short-sale conditioning and generally conservative nature make for prompt short covering. A few downticks will do nicely.

Another reason there may be so few short sellers around is that everyone likes a buyer, especially brokers. A buyer is optimistic and generally cheerful, almost by definition. And who needs a flock of sour faces sitting around cluttering up the boardroom, not only waiting but hoping for the market to crash? It's bad for business, and it keeps the ashtrays filled.

In spite of all the psychological obstacles to taking on short positions, I can't think of any legitimate reason for not doing so during periods of market weakness. Yet, throughout my earlier days in the stock market I was a perpetual optimist during both good times and bad. It escapes me now why anyone would fight all the prolonged downdrafts that inevitably occur even in bull markets. One of the most frustrating and repetitive scenarios I can recall consisted of nursing a stock along over a period of several weeks only to have it suddenly disintegrate in just a matter of days. This sawtooth action quickly became one of my least favorite chart patterns. Nevertheless, it points up a market characteristic that is certainly readily apparent if not altogether real. In my experience, downside action always seems to be overly severe and compressed into shorter time periods when compared with offsetting upside action. This statement, however, may be more accurate for individual price movement than the market in general. In any case, if this assumption is true, then with proper timing a negative market posture should produce the largest gains of all. Furthermore, if the market vehicle employed possessed the added leverage inherent in stock options, then a launch into the financial stratosphere would receive an added boost.

I find it difficult to fault any investor who refrains from short selling in the stock market or who is too timid to write naked options—although, for reasons already stated, I'm convinced the concern over abnormal risk is not warranted. On the contrary, high risk is better associated with being long in anything other than strong markets. It's the perpetual bull who lives dangerously with his capital resources, and he usually has the ulcers and yesterday's heartburn to show for it.

Perhaps the best answer to actively participating in bear market environments lies in the use of put options. When these investment vehicles are finally offered on the listed option exchanges, the psychological barriers to assuming a negative market posture will be lifted. No longer will the investor be subjected to unacceptable losses even if he freezes solid in the face of skyrocketing stock prices. The option price will set the maximum risk involved.

Without the benefit of past experience in trading listed put options, I believe some comments on the subject are still appropriate. In particular, for a strategy with maximum leverage, the guidelines of chapter 8 can be restated for put options as follows: *Buy near-term, far-out-of-the-money put options in negative market environments. The underlying stocks should be actively traded, volatile issues in depressed industry groups.*

A far-out-of-the-money put option is one where the underlying stock price is already well above the exercise price. Until the stock price falls and reaches the exercise price the option has no intrinsic value. This factor coupled with the near-term aspect of the option leads to low premiums and related advantages which have already been discussed (see chapter 7).

In the option selection process the underlying stock should be an actively traded, volatile issue capable of making large moves quickly to the downside. This usually implies selecting a stock that is exceptionally weak technically and has a correspondingly unfavorable chart pattern. Weak fundamentals may also be helpful if they are discernable and not already fully discounted. Professional money managers who drive up prices of their select group of favorite stocks on high volume and short notice often carry out the reverse action with even greater speed and vigor. When the romance with a security is over, yesterday's favorite quickly becomes today's outcast.

Generally, the underlying stock of a put option should also be a member in good standing of a depressed, or weak, industry group. Both stock and industry should be under distribution and the heavier the better. Measures of distribution are available from a number of market services including the *Trade Levels Report;* individual stocks may also be evaluated by the procedures discussed in chapter 9. For an additional thought on this matter, I suspect that industry group evaluation may play a more important role in selecting put options than with calls.

The timing of put options purchases should coincide with a negative market environment for maximum results. However, some anticipatory buying may also be appropriate prior to the end of calendar quarters if the market is not rising. The reasons for anticipating downside action are similar to those presented earlier and, if the expected downside price action does not materialize quickly, positions should be closed without delay.

The indicators of chapter 9 should be more than adequate for identifying negative market environments suitable for trading put options. Action signals provided by confirmation of the Summation Index and Tick Summation can be used to separate periods of market strength and weakness. In particular, sell signals generated by these indicators flash a green light for the purchase of put options; when a return of market strength is subsequently confirmed all positions should be closed.

There is a slight built-in market bias favoring the purchase of put rather than call options. It's generally recognized that it takes some measure of positive force just to keep the market on an even keel. Otherwise, stock prices tend to sink under the natural gravity of daily trading. No one is ever forced to purchase a security, but in the normal course of events people do find it necessary to liquidate assets and convert to cash. This type of activity produces a downward bias to stock prices and hence it works in favor of put options. The advantage may be slight, but it comes with the territory.

Many of the comments on diversification, selling principles, etc. discussed in chapter 8 apply equally to put options. They should be reviewed periodically whenever one is actively trading either type of option, put or call. After sufficient experience is gained working with puts, the trading guidelines may well require modification. It may even be beneficial to combine strategies and use both types of option. But with the inclusion of put options on the listed exchanges, the aggressive investor can indeed become a trader for all seasons.

Bibliography

Little Guy's Minilibrary

Below are a number of selections from my relatively small investment library. If it's true that you are what you eat, then these references were certainly part of the literary stew responsible for shaping my investment decisions. The selections are not listed in any particular order and are followed by brief comments.

● Gerald M. Loeb. *The Battle for Investment Survival.* New York: Simon & Schuster, 1965.

A classic book on the market written by a true elder statesman of the street, it's must reading for any serious investor. It covers a wide range of topics with appropriate depth.

● Gerald M. Loeb. *The Battle for Stock Market Profits.* New York: Simon & Schuster, 1971.

This effort is a must. It is like Loeb's earlier book above in both style and subject matter. Although it may seem a bit redundant, the material covered is of such significance that several readings are justified.

99

- Richard Ney. *The Wall Street Jungle.* New York: Grove Press, 1970.

Ney writes a reverse whodunit. He can't wait to tell you exactly who's responsible for all those silly ol' losses. He not only alerts one to the conspiracy on Wall Street but shows how to chart and predict when the big boys are going to reap wholesale and sow retail. But whether or not you're receptive to this particular brand of loser therapy, the book is informative on the inner workings of the market, especially the specialist system. It's worth cracking the canvas.

- Richard Ney. *The Wall Street Gang.* New York: Praeger, 1974.

This could be the *Wall Street Jungle* above in drag. Unless you really thrive on this conspiracy angle, one dose is probably enough. Use only as a booster shot.

- William L. Jiler. *How Charts Can Help You in the Stock Market.* New York: Trendline, 1970.

An excellent elementary reference book for identifying chart patterns, it's proved more than adequate for my attempts at technical analysis.

- Yale Hirsch. *The 197X Stock Traders Almanac.* Old Tappan, N.J.: The Hirsch Organization, 1972.

An annual publication that contains a wealth of historical market data and a variety of technical timing tools. In particular it includes data on seasonal trading patterns which can be especially useful for applying the options guidelines of chapter 7. The extensive overall collection of generally interesting facts and market pointers makes this almanac a prime item in anyone's library.

- William X. Scheinman. *Why Most Investors Are Mostly Wrong Most of the Time.* New York: Weybright and Talley, 1970.

I consider this book most suitable for the small investor who's definitely past the novice stage. It contains at least two very important chapters that discuss the influence of the money supply on the market and divergence analysis.

- Morton Shulman. *Anyone Can Make a Million.* New York: McGraw-Hill, 1966.

Shulman covers the gamut of investment possibilities from stocks and bonds to real estate and antiques. It's interesting reading, as it usually is when told by someone who's already made it to the winners circle.

- Lewis Owen. *How Wall Street Doubles My Money Every Three Years.* New York: Bernard Geis Associates, 1969.

I've never read a more entertaining book on the stock market that also had some sound general advice for the small investor. It contains an extensive glossary of market terms.

- Adam Smith. *The Money Game.* New York: Random House, 1968.

This is a most entertaining discussion on the human side of the stock market. It's written with humor and a perceptible dash of disrespect for the pompous buzzwords and jargon of Wall Street.

- Conrad W. Thomas. *Hedgemanship.* Homewood, Ill.: Dow Jones-Irwin, 1970.

If hedging your bets with both long and short positions is in your game plan, then this book may prove useful. Since I never could muster the courage to short stocks, this book has always remained the newest entry in my library.

- Curtis R. Richmond. *The Money Machine.* Glendale, Calif.: Church Press, 1972.

The author presents a stock market strategy based on the use of mutual funds as the investment vehicle. My general dislike of funds has never wavered, but this book does have some interesting market discussion on business cycles and technical analysis.

- Sam Shulsky. *Stock Buying Guide.* Greenwich, Conn.: Fawcett Publications, 1959.

This is the little paperback number that launched my stock market debut. It's seventy-five cents worth of nostalgia that has a permanent home in my minilibrary.

Optionable Stocks

As of January 1, 1977, there were 202 optionable stocks with options trading on the CBOE (C) plus the American (A), Philadelphia (P), Pacific (PC), and Midwest (M) Exchanges. They are listed below together with stock symbol, option series and trading Exchange(s).

Stock	Symbol	Exchange(s)	Series
AMF, Inc.	AMF	A	Feb.
AMP, Inc.	AMP	C	Feb.
ASA, Ltd.	ASA	A	Feb.
Abbott Laboratories	ABT	P	Feb.
Aetna Life & Casualty Co.	AET	A	Jan.
Allied Chemical Corp.	ACD	P	Jan.
Allis-Chalmers Corp.	AHG	P	Jan.
Aluminum Co. of America	AA	C	Jan.
Amerada Hess Corp.	AHC	P	Feb.

Stock	Symbol	Exchange(s)	Series
American Broadcasting Co., Inc.	ABC	PC	Feb.
American Cyanamid Co.	ACY	A	Jan.
American Electric Power Co., Inc.	AEP	C	Feb.
American Home Products Corp.	AHP	A	Jan.
American Hospital Supply Corp.	AHS	C	Feb.
American Telephone & Telegraph Co.	T	C	Jan.
Asarco, Inc.	AR	A	Jan.
Ashland Oil, Inc.	ASH	P	Jan.
Atlantic Richfield Co.	ARC	C	Jan.
Avnet, Inc.	AVT	A	Feb.
Avon Products, Inc.	AVP	C	Jan.
BankAmerica Corp.	BAM	C,PC	Jan.
Baxter Travenol Laboratories	BAX	C	Feb.
Beatrice Foods Co.	BRY	A	Jan.
Bethlehem Steel Corp.	BS	C	Jan.
Black & Decker Manufacturing Co.	BDK	C	Feb.
Boeing Co.	BA	C	Feb.
Boise Cascade Corp.	BCC	C,P	Feb.
Braniff International Corp.	BNF	P	Jan.
Bristol-Myers Co.	BMY	M	Mar.
Brunswick Corp.	BC	C	Jan.
Burlington Northern, Inc.	BNI	C	Jan.
Burroughs Corp.	BGH	A	Jan.
CBS, Inc.	CBS	C	Feb.
Carrier Corp.	CRR	M	Mar.
Caterpillar Tractor Co.	CAT	A	Feb.
Champion International Corp.	CHA	M	Mar.
Chase Manhattan Corp.	CMB	A	Jan.

Stock	Symbol	Exchange(s)	Series
Citicorp	FNC	C	Jan.
City Investing Co.	CNV	P	Jan.
Clorox Co.	CLX	P,PC	Jan.
Coca-Cola Co.	KO	C	Feb.
Colgate-Palmolive Co.	CL	C	Feb.
Commonwealth Edison Co.	CWE	C,P	Feb.
Communications Satellite Corp.	CQ	P	Jan.
Consolidated Edison Co. of New York	ED	A	Feb.
Continental Oil	CLL	P	Jan.
Continental Telephone Corp.	CTC	A	Jan.
Control Data Corp.	CDA	C	Feb.
Corning Glass Works	GLW	M	Mar.
Crown Zellerbach Corp.	ZB	PC	Jan.
Deere & Co.	DE	A	Jan.
Delta Air Lines, Inc.	DAL	C	Jan.
Diamond Shamrock Corp.	DIA	PC	Jan.
Digital Equipment Corp.	DEC	A	Jan.
Disney (Walt) Productions	DIS	A	Jan.
Dr. Pepper Co.	DOC	A	Feb.
Dow Chemical Co.	DOW	C	Jan.
Dresser Industries, Inc.	DI	P	Jan.
Dupont (E.I.) DeNemours & Co.	DD	A	Jan.
Duke Power Co.	DUK	P	Jan.
Eastern Gas & Fuel Associates	EFU	P	Jan.
Eastman Kodak Co.	EK	C	Jan.
El Paso Co.	ELG	A	Feb.
Engelhard Minerals & Chemicals Corp.	ENG	P	Jan.
Exxon Corp.	XON	C	Jan.
Federal National Mortgage Association	FNM	C	Jan.

Stock	Symbol	Exchange(s)	Series
Federated Department Stores, Inc.	FDS	PC	Feb.
Firestone Tire & Rubber Corp.	FIR	P	Feb.
First Charter Financial Corp.	FCF	A	Jan.
Fleetwood Enterprises	FLE	A	Feb.
Fluor Corp.	FLR	C	Jan.
Ford Motor Co.	F	C	Jan.
Freeport Minerals Co.	FT	M	Mar.
GAF Corp.	GAF	P	Jan.
General Dynamics Corp.	GD	C	Feb.
General Electric Co.	GE	C	Jan.
General Foods Corp.	GF	C	Feb.
General Motors Corp.	GM	C	Jan.
General Telephone & Electronics Corp.	GTE	A	Jan.
Georgia-Pacific Co.	GP	P	Jan.
Gillette Co.	GS	A	Jan.
Goodyear Tire & Rubber Co.	GT	A	Jan.
Grace (W.R.) & Co.	GRA	A	Feb.
Great Western Financial Corp.	GWF	C	Jan.
Greyhound Corp.	G	A	Jan.
Gulf & Western Industries, Inc.	GW	C	Jan.
Gulf Oil	GO	A	Jan.
Halliburton Co.	Hal	C	Jan.
Hercules, Inc.	HPC	A	Jan.
Heublein, Inc.	HBL	PC	Feb.
Hewlett-Packard Co.	HWP	C	Feb.
Hilton Hotels Corp.	HLT	PC	Feb.
Holiday Inns, Inc.	HIA	C	Feb.
Homestake Mining Co.	HM	C	Jan.

Stock	Symbol	Exchange(s)	Series
Honeywell, Inc.............	HON	C	Feb.
Household Finance Corp. ...	HFC	A	Jan.
Houston Oil & Minerals Corp....................	HOI	C,PC	Jan.
Howard Johnson Co........	HJ	P	Jan.
INA Corp................	INA	C	Jan.
International Business Machines Corp.	IBM	C	Jan.
International Flavors & Fragrances, Inc.	IFF	C	Feb.
International Harvester	HR	C	Jan.
International Minerals & Chemicals Corp..........	IGL	C	Jan.
International Paper Co......	IP	C	Jan.
International Telephone & Telegraph Corp.	ITT	C	Jan.
Jim Walter	JWC	C	Feb.
Johns-Manville Corp.......	JM	C	Feb.
Johnson & Johnson	JNJ	C	Jan.
Joy Manufacturing Co......	JOY	P	Feb.
Kennecott Copper Corp.	KN	C	Jan.
Kerr-McGee Corp..........	KMG	C	Jan.
Kresge (S.S.) Co...........	KG	C	Jan.
Levi Strauss & Co.	LVI	PC	Jan.
Lilly (Eli) & Co.	LLY	A	Jan.
Litton Industries, Inc.	LIT	M	Mar.
Loews Corp.	LTR	C	Jan.
Louisiana Land & Exploration Co...........	LLX	P	Feb.
Louisiana-Pacific Corp.	LPX	A	Feb.
MGIC Investment Corp.....	MGI	C,A	Feb.
Marriott Corp.	MHS	P	Feb.
McDermott (J. Ray) & Co., Inc.	MDE	P	Feb.
McDonald's Corp.	MCD	C	Jan.

Stock	Symbol	Exchange(s)	Series
McDonnell Douglas Corp.	MD	PC	Feb.
Merck & Co., Inc..........	MRK	C	Jan.
Merrill Lynch & Co., Inc.	MER	A,PC	Jan.
Mesa Petroleum Co.	MSA	A	Jan.
Middle South Utilities, Inc...	MSU	M	Mar.
Minnesota Mining & Manufacturing Co........	MMM	C	Jan.
Mobil Corp...............	MOB	C	Feb.
Monsanto Co.	MTC	C	Jan.
Morgan, J. P., & Co., Inc...	JPM	PC	Jan.
Motorola, Inc.............	MOT	A	Jan.
NCR Corp.	NCR	C	Jan.
National Distillers and Chemical Corp..........	DR	A	Feb.
National Semiconductor Corp...................	NSM	C	Feb.
Northwest Airlines, Inc.....	NWA	C	Jan.
Northwest Industries, Inc...	NWT	M	Mar.
Norton Simon, Inc.	NSI	A	Feb.
Occidental Petroleum Corp...	OXY	C	Feb.
Owens-Illinois, Inc.	OI	M	Mar.
PPG Industries, Inc.	PPG	P	Feb.
Penney, J.C., Co., Inc.	JCP	A	Feb.
Pennzoil Co.	PZL	C	Jan.
Pepsico, Inc.	PEP	C	Jan.
Pfizer, Inc................	PFE	A	Jan.
Phelps Dodge Corp........	PD	A	Jan.
Philip Morris, Inc.	MO	A	Jan.
Phillips Petroleum Co.......	P	A	Feb.
Pittston Co...............	PCO	P	Feb.
Polaroid Corp.............	PRD	C,PC	Jan.
Procter & Gamble Co.	PG	A	Jan.
RCA Corp.	RCA	C,PC	Jan.
Raytheon Co.	RTN	C	Feb.
Reserve Oil & Gas Co......	RVO	A	Feb.

Stock	Symbol	Exchange(s)	Series
Revlon, Inc.	REV	M	Mar.
Reynolds (R.J.) Industries, Inc.	RJR	C	Feb.
Reynolds Metals Co.	RLM	PC	Feb.
Rite Aid Corp.	RAD	A	Jan.
Rockwell International Corp.	ROK	M	Mar.
Safeway Stores, Inc.	SA	M	Mar.
Sambo's Restaurants, Inc. . . .	SRI	PC	Jan.
Santa Fe International Corp.	SAF	PC	Jan.
Schering-Plough Corp.	SGP	PC	Feb.
Schlumberger, Ltd.	SLB	C	Feb.
Scott Paper Co.	SPP	P	Jan.
Searle (G.D.) & Co.	SRL	A	Feb.
Sears, Roebuck and Co.	S	C	Jan.
Simplicity Pattern Co., Inc. . .	SYP	A	Feb.
Skyline Corp.	SKY	C	Feb.
Southern Co.	SO	C	Feb.
Sperry Rand Corp.	SY	C	Jan.
Standard Oil Co. of California	SD	A	Jan.
Standard Oil Co. (Indiana). .	SN	C	Feb.
Sterling Drug, Inc.	STY	A	Feb.
Sun Co., Inc.	SUN	P	Feb.
Syntex Corp.	SYN	C	Jan.
TRW Inc.	TRW	A	Jan.
Tandy Corp.	TAN	A	Jan.
Teledyne, Inc.	TDY	P	Jan.
Tenneco, Inc.	TGT	A	Feb.
Tesoro Petroleum Co.	TSO	C	Jan.
Texaco, Inc.	TX	A	Jan.
Texas Instruments, Inc.	TXN	C	Jan.
Texasgulf, Inc.	TG	C	Feb.
Tiger International, Inc.	TGR	A	Feb.
Transamerica Corp.	TA	P	Feb.
Travelers Corp.	TIC	PC	Feb.

Stock	Symbol	Exchange(s)	Series
UAL Inc.	UAL	C	Feb.
Union Carbide Corp.	UK	A	Jan.
Union Oil Co. of California	UCL	PC	Jan.
United States Steel Corp.	X	A,PC	Jan.
United Technologies Corp.	UTX	C	Feb.
Upjohn Co.	UPJ	C	Jan.
Virginia Electric and Power Co.	VEL	P	Jan.
Warner-Lambert Co.	WLA	A	Jan.
Western Union Corp.	WU	P	Jan.
Westinghouse Electric Corp.	WX	A	Jan.
Weyerhaeuser	WY	C	Jan.
Williams Co.	WMB	C	Feb.
Woolworth (F.W.) Co.	Z	P	Feb.
Xerox Corp.	XRX	C,PC	Jan.
Zenith Radio Corp.	ZE	A	Feb.

Index